10/23/09

UKRAINE

Volodymyr Bassis & Sakina Dhilawala

 **Marshall Cavendish** Benchmark

New York

PICTURE CREDITS
Cover photo: © Sean Sprague / The Image Works
age fotostock/ Bruno Morandi: 6, 59 • age footstock/ Ivan Vdovin: 36 • age fotostock/ Sean Sprague: 122 • age fotostock/
Wojtek Buss: 48 • alt.TYPE/ Reuters: 28, 49, 50, 52, 53, 88 • Andes Press Agency: 13, 65, 68, 72, 73, 74, 75, 78, 82, 83, 84, 97,
99, 119, 121 • Audrius Tomonis: 135 • Bjorn Klingwall: 15, 17, 35, 40, 58, 85 • Candella Advertising Agency Ltd: 11, 12, 19,
22, 26, 29, 30, 32, 37, 38, 41, 60, 64, 91, 93, 95, 101, 105, 109, 111, 120, 129 • Hulton Deutsch: 21, 24 • Hutchison Library:
86, 124 • Photolibrary/ Alamy: 1, 5, 14, 46, 54, 66, 80, 98, 106, 114, 116, 130 • Robert Semeniuk: 3, 4, 7, 8, 10, 42, 43, 44, 56,
57, 61, 62, 67, 70, 77, 81, 89, 100, 107, 108, 110, 112, 113, 118, 123, 125, 126, 127 • Stockfood/ Newedel, Karl: 131 • Susanna
Burton: 55, 79, 87, 103, 104, 115 • The Image Bank: 33, 94

PRECEDING PAGE
Ukrainians in traditional dress

Publisher (U.S.): Michelle Bisson
Editors: Deborah Grahame, Mabelle Yeo, Crystal Ouyang
Copyreader: Daphne Hougham
Designer: Rachel Chen
Cover picture researcher: Connie Gardner
Picture researcher: Thomas Khoo

Marshall Cavendish Benchmark
99 White Plains Road
Tarrytown, NY 10591
Web site: www.marshallcavendish.us

© Times Editions Private Limited 1997
© Marshall Cavendish International (Asia) Private Limited 2009
All rights reserved. First edition 1997. Second edition 2009.
® "Cultures of the World" is a registered trademark of Times Publishing Limited.

Originated and designed by Times Editions Private Limited
An imprint of Marshall Cavendish International (Asia) Private Limited
A member of Times Publishing Limited

All Internet sites were correct and accurate at the time of printing. All monetary figures in this publication are in U.S. dollars.

Library of Congress Cataloging-in-Publication Data
Bassis, Volodymyr.
    Ukraine / by Volodymyr Bassis & Sakina Dhilawala. — 2nd ed.
      p. cm. — (Cultures of the world (2nd ed.))
    Summary: "Provides comprehensive information on the geography, history, wildlife, governmental structure, economy,
      cultural diversity, peoples, religion, and culture of Ukraine"—Provided by publisher.
    Includes bibliographical references and index.
      ISBN 978-0-7614-2090-3
    1. Ukraine—Juvenile literature. I. Dhilawala, Sakina, 1964– II. Title. III. Series.
    DK508.515.B37 2007
    947.7—dc22   2007019179

Printed in China

9 8 7 6 5 4 3 2 1

CONTENTS

**A Ukrainian boy giving
his baby brother a ride in
a horse-drawn cart.**

Clothes hanging out to
dry in the warm autumn
sunshine.

INTRODUCTION

UKRAINE IS LOCATED in the heart of Eastern Europe, with borders on seven neighboring countries and the Black Sea. The history of Ukraine is one of continuous struggle for independence from one after another of these next-door powers . In 1991 this dream, fostered for centuries, finally became reality. Today Ukraine is politically independent, an equal member of the world's commonwealth of states, and endeavoring to build a democratic society.

As with many of the former Soviet Union countries, Ukraine inherited an economy based on heavy industry and technology. The country's foremost challenge since its independence has been to diversify and step aside from many of the industry-based economies that relied heavily on governmental subsidies.

Given that it is one of the largest countries in Europe, with some of the most fertile soil in the world, and considering the hardworking and peace-loving nature of its people, Ukraine will undoubtedly become one of the most prosperous nations of the 21st century.

GEOGRAPHY

UNTIL 1991 UKRAINE was part of the Union of Soviet Socialist Republics (USSR). Today it is a proudly independent state located in southeastern Europe. The land area of Ukraine is 233,090 square miles (603,700 square km), making Ukraine the largest country situated completely in Europe. France is only slightly smaller, and the state of Texas only slightly larger. To the north, Ukraine borders Belarus; to the northeast, Russia. Turkey and Bulgaria are just across the Black Sea in the south, while Moldova, Romania, Hungary, Slovakia, and Poland lie to the west and southwest.

Ukraine's geographical position brought the country under the influence of many different cultures and civilizations. Once the country was freed from foreign rule, Ukrainians have been able to make use of their remarkable natural resources of climate, minerals, and soil.

Left: **Neatly cared-for countryside around the village of Verhna, near Lviv.**

Opposite: **The cliff-top Swallow's Nest castle outside Yalta on Ukraine's Crimean Peninsula gives visitors a stunning view of the Black Sea.**

In southwestern Ukraine, the foothills slowly rise until they meet the Carpathian Mountains.

GEOGRAPHICAL REGIONS

There are no domestic borders on the administrative map of Ukraine indicating the end of eastern Ukraine and the beginning of western. There are distinctions, however, among central, eastern, southern, and western Ukraine and the Crimea, located on a peninsula in the Black Sea. Geographically Ukraine is divided into two major regions by a line running from the southwest of the country to the northeast. The line crosses the Dnipro River approximately halfway between Kiev (also spelled Kyiv) and Dnipropetrovsk.

The southern zone of the country is drier than the rest, with a predominantly continental climate and steppe vegetation. The northern zone is characterized by deciduous or mixed forest vegetation with a moist and cooler climate.

More than 70 percent of Ukraine's total land area is used for general agricultural purposes. During the last glacial period, the entire country was covered with a layer of loamy loess, which is the basis of the thick, black, fertile soil throughout the country.

RIVERS

Several rivers carve their paths through the Carpathian Mountains in the west, including the Tysa, the Cheremosh, the Stryy, and the Dnister. The Dnister River is one of the fastest flowing rivers in Europe, running for 876 miles (1,409 km), almost entirely in Ukraine, before it empties into the Black Sea. The Dnipro River follows nearly the same route in the east. It is the largest river in Ukraine, running south from its source in Russia for 1,420 miles (2,285 km) until it, too, reaches the Black Sea, near the city of Kherson. The Dnipro is to Ukraine what the Nile and Amazon rivers are to Egypt and Brazil. It is important as a passenger, tourist, and cargo waterway. Its main tributaries are the Pryp'yat and Desna rivers. The Danube River runs along the southwestern border, separating Ukraine and Romania. The Pivdennyy (or Southern Bug) is a large river that courses through central Ukraine.

CLIMATE

Ukraine has a moderate continental climate with four distinct seasons and a comparatively consistent landscape and gradual temperature changes that keep the country out of the path of weather extremes like tornadoes and hurricanes.

In northern Ukraine, cooler weather with temperatures around 30°F (-1°C) and occasional snow may start as early as the middle of October and last right into the month of March. Altitude plays an important role in the Carpathian and Crimean mountains, lowering temperatures and increasing precipitation as it changes, while, in the coastal areas, the waters of the Black Sea and Sea of Azov cause a definite tempering effect. In the Crimea, summer begins in early May and lasts until late September. There is little snow in winter. In the Carpathians, the

Sunflowers are one of the primary crops grown in Ukraine. Sunflowers are very valuable because the leaves are used for live-stock food, the flowers for dye, and the seeds for cooking oil and snacks.

climate is somewhat cooler, with a winter average of 25°F (-4°C), and warm, pleasant summers of 75°F–80°F (24°C–27°C). If the temperature gets higher than 85°F (29°C), it is considered extremely hot. Such excessive summer heat never lasts for more than a week, though. Long and comfortable springs and autumns are the most enjoyable seasons in Ukraine.

FLORA

Ukraine is proud of its rich vegetation of more than 30,000 types of plants and trees. Expanses of pine and deciduous trees such as oak make up a good part of the forests that enrich the country. About 30 percent of Ukraine's territory is covered by forests, meadows, and steppes. Many varieties of flowers and herbs thrive in Ukrainian forests, fields, and mountains, and many of the country's invaluable medicinal flora species are used in the preparation of important medicines.

The Crimean and Carpathian mountains are homes to the largest number of endemic plant species in Ukraine. As found in the other parts of the world, however, undesirable human intervention and expanding urban development have both altered the natural landscape and adversely affected the plant biodiversity in Ukraine. Still, the creation and maintenance of national parks and natural reserves have helped the country's efforts in the conservation of its forests. Some of the best-known natural preserves are Medobory, Polisskyy, Yaltynskyy, and one on the Dunai River. As early as 1921 a biosphere preservation project called Askania-Nova was set in motion and national natural parks Azovo-Syvaskyy, Shatskyy, and Synevyr were declared protected zones. Today there are 15 nature and four biosphere reserves, eight national natural parks, and 17 botanical gardens.

FAUNA

Wildlife in Ukraine is typical of steppes—level, treeless prairie tracts—and forest areas. Centuries ago bears and wolves roamed the forests, but today the largest predator is the red fox, which can be seen in almost all the woodlands of the country, along with lesser numbers of wild boar and deer. Smaller animals include badgers, hares, red squirrels, and hedgehogs.

The red fox prefers to live in farmlands and wood-lots, making the country-side of Ukraine a veritable red fox paradise.

Rivers and lakes are the habitat for muskrat, otter, coypu (a semiaquatic rodent), and beaver. In the steppes, there are gophers and other small rodents. Ukraine has few snakes, although some venomous vipers are found in damp or swampy areas, as well as in burial mounds. There are also several varieties of harmless grass snakes and lizards.

The steppe eagle is one of the largest Ukrainian birds. Other birds of prey living in various regions of the country include hawks, falcons, and owls. Swallows, bluebirds, and sparrows are seen in abundance all over the country. In the past, bullfinches were common in the winter, but there are fewer now due to warmer winters and the widespread pollution of the environment. Wild and domestic pigeons are common in the cities, while in the forests there are magpies and cuckoos. Some lakes, ponds, and reed-covered riverbanks provide summer homes for a variety of ducks and geese.

Pike, perch, perch-pike, crucian, gudgeon, carp, and many other freshwater fish are common in the rivers, lakes, and ponds in Ukraine. The Black and Azov seas used to be significant sources for commercial fishing before overfishing in the 1950s diminished the fish resources drastically.

ADMINISTRATIVE DIVISIONS

Ukraine is divided into administrative units called *oblasts* (OB-lahsts), the equivalent of states in the United States. There are 24 *oblasts* and one autonomous republic—the Crimea. An *oblast* is a political territory with its own borders, government, and capital, called the *oblast* center, from which the name of the *oblast* is derived. For example, the capital city of Cherkaska Oblast in central Ukraine is Cherkasy. Each *oblast* is divided into counties called *rayons* (rai-OHNs).

CITIES

Ukraine is generally densely populated, and there are a significant number of large cities. In fact, there are four cities with populations over one million and some 32 with populations over 200,000. In Ukraine a city

Kreshchatik, Kiev's main thoroughfare, is the business and administrative heart of the city.

of fewer than 100,000 people would be described as small, and a settlement with under 5,000 people would not even be considered a town.

The capital of Ukraine is Kiev, with a population of approximately 2.6 million. Kiev was the center of Rus, a medieval East Slavic state. As the ancient capital of the Slavs, there are still numerous churches, monasteries, and monuments reflecting Kiev's golden age. Parliament, the president's headquarters, and the various ministries are all located in Kiev.

Other cities with populations over one million are Kharkiv, Dnipropetrovsk, and Donetsk in the east, Odessa (also spelled Odesa) in the south, and

A view of the city of Lviv, Ukraine's cosmopolitan western capital.

Lviv in the west. Lviv is called the "western capital" of Ukraine because during the repressive Soviet era it was in the west that Ukrainian culture survived. The city was built by the Ukrainian king Danylo Romanovych in the 13th century and named for his son Lev. Because of its location near the border, Lviv has a diverse population, architectural styles, and traditions, including Ukrainian, Polish, Jewish, Austrian, and Hungarian.

Kharkiv, the country's main industrial city, is the location of the National Academies of Science. Surrounding the city are large deposits of iron ore and coal, which are mined and processed in Kharkiv.

Dnipropetrovsk is another important industrial city, located along the banks of the Dnipro River. It is a busy river port and railroad junction.

The main seaport in Ukraine is Odessa, on the northwestern shore of the Black Sea. It is the site of a large shipbuilding industry and is a manufacturing and trading center. People living and working in this cosmopolitan city represent more than 100 nationalities.

HISTORY

UKRAINE HAS BEEN at the crossroads of migration, trade, and war for most of its 2,000-year history. Its fertile land has attracted numerous invaders throughout its existence. Today, for the first time in history, Ukraine's territories are united under one government.

THE EARLIEST DAYS

The first signs of people in the territory of modern Ukraine date back 150,000 years. In the late 19th century, excavations that took place in the village of Trypillia, not far from Kiev, uncovered evidence of a unique civilization dating from 4500 to 2000 B.C. It soon became known as the Trypillian civilization. Trypillians lived in communities of about 10,000 people, 15 or so individuals sharing two-story log houses, which they situated to form a large circle. Hunters and gatherers, the Trypillians also smelted bronze and produced mysteriously beautiful objects of art.

In the last millennium B.C., different groups of nomads—Cimmerians, Scythians, and Sarmatians—migrated to the southern part of modern Ukraine. The Scythians, especially, left traces of their life on the steppes near the Black Sea coasts. They were very accomplished equestrians and were among the first people to master the art of horseback riding. This mobility gave them a great advantage over their neighbors, enabling them to attack and infiltrate quickly. The Cimmerians, who still fought on foot, soon succumbed to the stronger Scythian cavalry and were forced to flee the plains north of the Black Sea. This series of victories brought great fame to the Scythians, who became very prosperous after settling in the plains. Scythian rulers were given grand burials. Grave sites discovered in the Crimea and other places on the steppe have yielded tombs filled

Above: **The remains of an ancient Scythian capital in Neopol Skifsky.**

Opposite: **A statue of Vladimir Lenin still stands in Yalta's town center.**

*Three brothers,
Kyi, Schek, and
Khoriv, are
the legendary
founders of Kiev.
The city was
named after the
oldest brother, Kyi.
Two parts of the
city, Schekovytsa
and Khorevytsa,
were named after
Schek and Khoriv.
The river was
named after their
sister Lybid.*

with gold and other precious metals. The Scythians enjoyed this wealth and power until the fourth century B.C., when the Sarmatians appeared on the scene. The Sarmatians ceaselessly put pressure on the Scythians, squeezing them southward until they were confined to the Crimea. These tireless invaders gradually supplanted the Scythians as the rulers of the steppe. By the second century B.C., they had destroyed the last remnants of this once powerful community.

THE SLAVS

To escape the invading Huns, the Slavs, direct ancestors of modern Ukrainians, moved south into the Black Sea area in the fifth century A.D. Slavs originally came from Asia, but migrated to eastern Europe in the third or second millennium B.C. In the fifth and sixth centuries A.D., the westward movement of the Germans stimulated the great migration of the Slavs into present-day Ukraine. They originally occupied the area between the Vistula and Dnipro rivers, stretching northward to the Carpathian Mountains. The Slavs began to expand their region, and by the end of the eighth century they had conquered the Balkans as well. The Hungarians occupied the eastern part of the Balkan Peninsula, but they were quickly assimilated into the Slavs. Both groups had converted to Christianity in the ninth century. An Asian invasion in the ninth century divided the southern Slavs from those of the west and east. The western Slavs (Czechs, Slovaks, Elbe Slavs, Poles, and Pomeranians) adopted Roman Catholicism, while the eastern Slavs (White Russians—in modern times, anticommunists mainly from Estonia, Latvia, and Lithuania—Russians, and Ukrainians) adhered to the Greek Orthodox Church.

KIEVAN RUS

According to legends in an early chronicle, *Tale of Bygone Years*, said to be written by a monk named Nestor in 1113, Kiev was founded in the seventh century A.D. by Prince Kyi and his family. The community in Kiev flourished until an attack by the Khazars devastated the territory. In the ninth century, Slavs, who by that time had settled in the region, called on Viking rulers from northern Europe to assist in the government of Kiev. The Viking rulers were later killed when Prince Oleg conquered Kiev in 882 A.D. This was to be the beginning of a line of rulers of the Rurik dynasty. At that time the people of Kiev were known as the Rus, so the new state established by the Ruriks was called Kievan Rus.

A mural portrait of Christian monks painted on a wall of the Lavra monastery in Kiev.

In the 10th century, Prince Volodymyr, the fourth member of the Rurik dynasty, became the first Christian ruler of Kievan Rus. Although Christianity had existed in Kiev long before Volodymyr's time, he had remained a pagan. In 988 Volodymyr embraced Christianity when he married the sister of Byzantine emperor Basil II. In that year, he ordered the Christian conversion of Kiev in a move to unite the Slavic peoples in the region.

Volodymyr's son, Prince Yaroslav, also promoted Christianity as the religion of the Slavs. He built schools and churches, established written laws, and forged ties with neighboring nations by marrying his three sons and three daughters into other royal families. Through his military victories, Yaroslav consolidated the Kievan state and made Kievan Rus into the largest empire in Europe.

STRUGGLE FOR POWER, DEFENSE AGAINST INVADERS

After Yaroslav's death, there was a struggle for power among his three sons. The country was divided into three principalities ruled by his offspring, which made it easy prey for invaders, particularly the nomad tribes of the Polovtsy. From 1057 to 1100 Kievan Rus suffered again and again from Polovtsy invasions, which saw Kiev's decline and the end of the golden period of political stability achieved by Volodymyr and carried on by his son, Yaroslav. During the same period, there was a major shift in trade routes, brought on by the First Crusade, making the route between the Baltic and Black seas superfluous.

In 1223 the Mongols invaded. By that time, the principalities had been at war intermittently for generations, and the Mongols' mounted warriors were too skillful for the weakened Slavs to repel.

After the defeat of the Slavs, the Mongols established a unified political system in an attempt to revive the commerce that had traditionally crossed the Central Asian plains. Although much of the country lay in ruins due to years of fighting, many cities made a surprisingly rapid recovery under the rule of the Mongols. Kiev, however, never fully regained its grandeur. Administration of the principalities was left in the hands of the Turkic leaders and Muslim merchants who had been operating in the area for generations.

In 1241 the Mongols founded the Golden Horde, a state that extended from the Danube River to the Ural River and at its height included areas such as the Crimea, Bulgaria, Moldova, and parts of Siberia. To avoid further conquest, Ukrainians moved westward and established the state of Galicia-Volhynia. The state remained independent until 1340, when it succumbed to the superior powers of Lithuania and Poland. From the

KOZAKS

Originally runaways from unbearable conditions of life under the landlords, Kozaks formed democratic military communities on the Dnipro River islands. They elected their leaders, lived a life of constant training, and fought against the Tatars, Turks, Poles, and Russians. Later, they even fought for the Russians. History books and folk songs praise the names of prominent

Kozak leaders, called *hetman* (HET-mahn) in Ukrainian, such as Yevstafiy Dashkevych, Dmytro Vyshnevetskyy, Petro Sagaidachnyy, and Mykhailo Doroshenko. Despite many attempts to disband the Kozaks, the active movement persisted until the 18th century, with Kozak units serving in the Russian army. Eventually many settled down and began farming and raising horses.

1340s on, much of Ukraine came under the sovereignty of the Grand Duchy of Lithuania. Yet Ukrainian territories under Lithuania maintained much of their political and cultural self-determination.

In the 1380s the Lithuanian-Polish contest for power over Galicia-Volhynia ended when Lithuania annexed Volhynia and Poland established legitimate control over Galicia. Lithuania was united with Poland in 1385 by a matrimonial union between Lithuania's Grand Duke Jogaila and Poland's Queen Jadwiga. This marriage created a dynastic union of the two powers. When Lithuania and Poland were constitutionally united by the 1569 Union of Lublin, western Ukraine and the city of Kiev came under the control of the Polish king. As Polish subjects, Ukrainians were required to learn the Polish language and to adopt Roman Catholicism, the Polish faith.

At that time there were numerous Ukrainian uprisings against their Polish and Lithuanian occupiers. Many peasants escaped from their landlords and led dangerous, but free, lives. These hardy fugitives were called *Kozaks* (koh-ZAHK, Cossacks in English spelling), a name that is derived from the Turkish word for "a free man."

17TH-CENTURY UKRAINE

The strong Kozak army and the system of Hetmanship brought revival to the Ukrainian people and their culture. The Kozak troops made many successful raids on Moscow and in the Crimea in the early 1600s and fought with the Polish army and the Tatars. The position of the leader of the Orthodox church, the patriarch, was restored in 1620, and the first institute for higher learning, called the Kievan Academy, was founded by Petro Mohyla in 1632.

Besides the regular raids against Poland, several anti-Polish uprisings took place in different parts of Ukraine in 1630, 1635, and 1638. One prominent Kozak leader, Bohdan Khmelnytskyy, organized an anti-Polish movement that triumphed in several battles but never completely defeated the Polish army. In 1654 Khmelnytskyy signed the Pereyaslav Treaty, uniting Ukraine with Russia, in an effort to oust the Poles from power. The united Kozak-Russian army was a powerful fighting force. The Kozaks soon realized, however, that while fighting one oppressor, they appeared to be falling under the thumb of another, even stronger one—Russia.

In 1708 the leader of the Kozak army, Hetman Ivan Mazepa, left the Russian army and joined Swedish king Karl XII. In the ensuing battle at Poltava, the Swedish-Kozak army was defeated by the Russians, which set the stage for the Russian colonization of Ukraine.

UKRAINE IN THE RUSSIAN EMPIRE

Peter the Great, the czar of Russia, ruled his empire with an iron fist. Decrees limiting Ukrainian freedom were issued from the outset. The second part of the century saw the further colonization of Ukraine, with Russia taking over former Polish and Austrian territories.

Red Guards shooting from an armored car in Petrograd (Saint Petersburg) in October 1917, the year of the Russian Revolution.

In the 19th century, the first signs of discontent became visible. A peasant movement for freedom began in 1813, a revolt by nobles (called Decembrists) in Kiev and Odessa took place in 1825, and prominent Ukrainians raised their voices to restore the rights of the Ukrainian people.

At the same time, coal deposits were first discovered in eastern Ukraine; the first sugar refineries were built in central Ukraine; the southern cities of Odessa and Mykolayiv were founded; and new universities opened their doors in Kharkiv, Kiev, and Odessa. Several magazines and newspapers were published in Ukrainian (despite the fact that it was forbidden) and were distributed both in Ukraine and abroad. In 1861, under the pressure of the uprisings and the wave of dissatisfaction, serfdom was abolished. Yulian Bachynskyy's article "Ukraina Irredenta," published in 1895, was the first public mention of Ukrainian independence.

SOVIET POWER IN UKRAINE

Poverty and hunger throughout the Russian Empire in the early 20th century, fueled a growing national liberation movement in Ukraine and a developing revolutionary faction in Russia. Communist revolutionaries wanted to establish a new kind of government in Russia and plotted to overthrow the czar. The leader of the Communists,

Joseph Stalin, strong-armed former head of the USSR.

Vladimir Lenin, promised peace, food, and land to the people. In March 1917 the Communists overthrew the czar. In November of that year, the Communists seized power in Saint Petersburg and Moscow, and the first Ukrainian National Republic was proclaimed in Kiev by the Third Ukrainian Universal Congress. In January 1918 the Fourth Universal Congress proclaimed Ukraine independent, with sovereign borders, its own currency, a constitution, and a government. The first president of the Ukrainian National Republic, Mykhailo Hrushevskyy, was elected in April 1918. Lenin's new Communist state, and several other nations, recognized Ukrainian independence.

The republic was short-lived, though, and with the advance of Soviet Russia's army in 1919, a full-scale civil war erupted, lasting for almost two years. Ukrainian nationals continued to strive for an independent Ukraine, but by the end of 1920 the "independent" Ukrainian Soviet Socialist Republic had been formed. Mikhail Bulgakov's novel *The White Guard* tells of this time in Kiev.

INTEGRATION INTO THE SOVIET UNION

According to the terms of a treaty between the Russian Soviet Socialist Federation and the Ukrainian Soviet Socialist Republic, signed in December 1920, both countries remained independent but formed an economic and military union. In reality, Ukraine had become Russia's milk cow, providing her with food, coal, and other necessities. Ukrainian culture, economy, and government were gradually pulled under Moscow's control, even more so after the formation of the Union of Soviet Socialist Republics (USSR) in December 1922.

Intensive industrialization of the eastern areas of Ukraine continued over the next 10 years, and strict measures were taken to reorganize agriculture. The new leader of the USSR, Joseph Stalin, abolished private farms and ordered the creation of state-run collective farms instead. Farmers were forced to give up their land and livestock and to work as hired labor on government farms. Those who protested were arrested, executed, or sent into exile.

WORLD WAR II

After the signing of the Molotov-Ribbentrop Pact in 1939, which banned any conflict between the USSR and Germany, both countries made vast territorial gains. The new borders were considered sovereign, but both countries were preparing for war. For Ukraine, the war started on June 22, 1941, with the German army invading its western borders and bombing Kiev. Despite the heroic defense of the major cities, all of Ukraine was occupied by July 1942. Some Ukrainians hailed the Germans as their liberators, but it soon became apparent that Ukraine had in no

It is estimated that about 8 million Ukrainian lives were lost as the result of World War II, including 4 million civilians killed and more than 2 million taken to Germany as forced labor.

FAMINE IN UKRAINE

Ukraine was one of the first areas in the USSR to be targeted for collectivization under Stalin's new agricultural program because it was a rich grain-producing region. Wealthy Ukrainian farmers, called *kulaks* (COO-lacks)—the Soviet label for those who owned a slightly larger than average plot of land and had hired labor—were exiled or executed. Anyone who actively resisted was also labeled *kulak* and suffered a similar fate. The transition caused terrible disruptions in production, but exorbitant taxes were still demanded from peasants. A drought in 1932–33 caused a famine in which millions died of starvation. The tragic depravation was exacerbated by the Soviets' collectivization agenda and their attempt to eliminate the *kulaks*, who had their land seized and were compelled into collectivization. Nearly 7 million Ukrainians starved to death in less than two years. Everything possible was done by the government to prevent the world from discovering what had really happened in Ukraine. And when they did discover something, they were discouraged from believing it.

The Conference of the Big Three (British Prime Minister Winston Churchill, President Franklin D. Roosevelt, and Premier Josef Stalin) as it is often referred to, took place at Yalta in February 1945.

way been liberated. In October 1942 the Ukrainian Resistance Army was created in Lviv. It confronted both the German and the Soviet armies in the hope of attaining Ukrainian independence. As early as December 1942, the Soviet army had started its counteroffensive. Ukraine was finally free from German occupation only in October 1944.

While restoration of Ukrainian industry and agriculture began immediately after the war, the restoration of its language and culture was still many years away.

MODERN UKRAINE

In 1985 new policies of perestroika (pair-a-STROY-ka, restructuring) and glasnost (GLASS-nost, openness) were introduced by the first, and to be the last, president of the USSR, Mikhail Gorbachev. These opportunities allowed the national renaissance in Ukraine to burst out. In April 1986 the Chernobyl nuclear-plant accident added tension to the political situation. For the first time in many years, in 1987, Ukraine celebrated a Christian event, the 1,000th anniversary of the Christianization of Ukraine.

A national democratic movement called *Rukh* ("movement" in Ukrainian) was founded in September 1989, and the authorities had to register it as a legal political organization in January 1990—a significant event in a country with a one-party system. Ukrainian became the official language in October 1989. Events of a similar nature were happening all over the Soviet Union.

In August 1991 an attempt by reactionary Communists to overthrow Gorbachev urged the majority of the republics that made up the Soviet

Union to ban the Communist Party. On August 24, 1991, the Ukrainian parliament declared Ukraine independent. A national referendum took place on December 1, 1991, and an overwhelming majority (about 90 percent) of Ukrainians voted for independence.

POST–SOVIET RULE

With independence came responsibility, and the new Ukrainian government faced a tough challenge in wresting away from Russia's economic influence and ensuring civil liberties and prosperity for its citizens. A difficult economic legacy, widespread corruption, and a lack of political agreement over reform led to a decade of economic decline.

The first president of independent Ukraine was Leonid Kravchuk (1991–94). During his term, Ukraine saw a sharp fall in industrial output and inflation ballooned. His successor, Leonid Kuchma, was equally powerless to change things. During his 10-year presidency (1994–2004), restructuring and bureaucratic reform were delayed due to greedy political and bureaucratic interests. In the 2004 presidential election, an increasing number of Ukrainians rallied under the former prime minister, Viktor Yushchenko, who was challenging the current prime minister supported by Kuchma, Viktor Yanukovich, for the presidential office. The campaign started out with Yushchenko clearly emerging as Ukraine's most popular candidate.

The contest between the political parties reached a climax after Yanukovich, contrary to all opinion polls, was declared the winner. Ukrainians cried foul and poured into the streets of Kiev to overturn what they saw as a rigged ballot. The dispute caught the attention of international audiences, with the European Union and the United States backing Yushchenko, and Russia openly supporting Kuchma's candidate,

Leonid Kuchma, the president of Ukraine from 1994 to 2004 was widely criticized in the West as a man with pro-Russian attitudes.

Yanukovich. In the end, the orange-clad pro-Yuschenko protesters emerged victorious after a rerun presidential election monitored by international observers. The Orange Revolution, as it became known, ushered in a new pro-Western reform-minded government led by Viktor Yushchenko.

As president, Yushchenko was determined to bring about radical political and economic changes. But although his government did make considerable progress on issues of freedom of the media and political freedom, efforts at confronting corruption and the socioeconomic situation have not been as successful as hoped.

Prime Minister Yuliya Tymoshenko (who was Yushchenko's important ally during the Orange Revolution) accused the Yushchenko administration of being too soft on the former Kuchma regime. Her criticism eventually led to her being ousted as prime minister.

In March 2006, Ukraine held its fourth parliamentary elections since independence. The elections were held according to the new system of proportional vote. Deputies to the parliament are now elected for five-year terms instead of four, and during their terms, they are not allowed to quit the party on whose ticket they ran.

Although Viktor Yanukovych's Party of Regions won the elections, it did not get enough votes to form a government on its own. On June 22, Ukraine's three major parties reached a coalition agreement, assigning the post of prime minister to Yuliya Tymoshenko and the post of deputy prime minister to the leader of the Socialist Party, Oleksandr Moroz.

The Party of Regions then staged a blockade of the parliament to protest its being excluded from the government. On July 6, when they lifted their blockade, Socialist Party leader Oleksandr Moroz, acting against the coalition agreement, nominated himself for the position of parliamentary speaker and was elected with the backing of the Party of Regions and the Communist Party.

Soon after Moroz's appointment as parliamentary speaker, a new coalition of the Party of Regions, the Socialist Party, and the Communist Party was announced. This time the Yuliya Tymoshenko bloc staged parliamentary blockades to prevent the coalition from being installed. The president's Our Ukraine party remained undecided.

After months of political deadlock, on August 4 President Yushchenko decided to appoint his former rival Viktor Yanukovych as prime minister.

The Orange Revolution was a great historical event for Ukraine, the Soviet Union, and all of Europe. While the concept of civil society was innate in Central Europe, it did not exist in the former Soviet republics. The Orange Revolution inspired Ukraine's youth with this concept and has become irreversible. It also changed the relationship Ukraine had with Russia from its being handheld to making its own mature, independent decisions.

Despite these changes, however, criticism of the Yushchenko government is more substantial than praise is supportive. Expectations of immediate, rapid, and comprehensive change after the Orange Revolution greatly outstripped the reality of the changes instituted by the Orange governments in 2005 and 2006. Though change for the better did occur, it was less than what the population had hoped for. Instead of a united coalition, Ukraine's political parties have been engaged in constant squabbling, as evident during the parliamentary elections. The Orange Revolution's primary promise to implement justice and empower the people has proven hollow. Many politicians accused of corruption are still in government.

GOVERNMENT

SINCE THE FALL OF THE SOVIET UNION, Ukraine has become an independent republic for the second time in its long history. Today, Ukrainians participate fully in the government of their country, taking advantage of the freedom to become involved in decisions affecting their land, their children, and their homes.

Now an active supporter of nuclear disarmament, Ukraine has refused to house nuclear weapons in its territory. The government attempts to resolve problems of all kinds peacefully and democratically.

LEGISLATION

The legislative body of the nation is the Supreme Council, or Verkhovna Rada (ver-KHOV-nah RAH-dah). The Verkhovna Rada is a unicameral parliament that enacts its decisions based on the votes of its members from various political parties.

Constitutional amendments aimed at significantly increasing parliament's power came into force on January 1, 2006. Under the amended constitution, parliament's term was increased from four to five years, and the prime minister is to be nominated as head of the executive branch through a parliamentary majority. The prime minister will then nominate members of his cabinet, who will have to be approved by parliament. The president, who formerly appointed the government and had the right to dismiss ministers, will now have only the right to propose the minister for foreign affairs and the defense minister.

Under the 2006 amended constitution, the Verkhovna Rada now has 450 members who are elected according to the proportional representation system. Previously, under the mixed system, 225 members were elected

Above: **Mariinsky Palace, the president's headquarters, is located in Kiev, as is the Verkhovna Rada, the parliament.**

Opposite: **Riot police stand guard near Ukraine's Constitutional Court as supporters of Prime Minister Viktor Yanukovich attend a rally near the court in Kiev.**

from single-member constituencies and the remaining 225 seats were filled using a proportional system. The Verkhovna Rada initiates legislation, ratifies international agreements, and approves the budget.

FEDERAL GOVERNMENT

Carrying out the laws and decrees of the Verkhovna Rada is the duty of the federal government, represented by the Cabinet of Ministers and the various ministries. The Cabinet of Ministers is under the control of and accountable to the Verkhovna Rada. It is guided in its activity by the constitution and the laws of Ukraine and by the acts of its president.

The first president of Ukraine, Leonid Kravchuk, was elected almost unanimously, since he was the chairman of the Verkhovna Rada and initiated Ukraine's independence decree in August 1991. He also supported the banning of the Communist Party, despite the fact that in Soviet Ukraine he occupied one of the top positions in the Ukrainian Communist Party.

Leonid Kravchuk became Ukraine's first president in 1991.

LAW AND ORDER

Direct enforcement of laws is handled by the *militsya* (mih-LIH-tsiah), the Ukrainian police, under the auspices of the Ministry of Home Affairs. Militiamen wearing dark blue uniforms and armed with handguns and clubs walk through the streets of Ukrainian cities or cruise in highway patrol cars. Recently, special militia forces armed with automatic weapons have also appeared.

VIKTOR YUSHCHENKO

Viktor Yushchenko was elected president of Ukraine in January 2005 after an eventful presidential election. Mr. Yushchenko had served as head of Ukraine's central bank, the National Bank of Ukraine, from 1993 to 1999, where he was instrumental in creating the country's national currency, the hryvnia, and in establishing a modern regulating system for commercial banking. In 1999 he was appointed prime minister by Leonid Kuchma.

During his short tenure as prime minister (1999–2001), he was credited with achieving significant economic progress for the country. Yushchenko's approach helped to turn around Ukraine's economy—in 2000, his first full year as prime minister, Ukraine's economy grew by nearly 6 percent, and in 2001 annual growth rose to 9.2 percent.

In 2001, despite Yushchenko's very credible achievements as prime minister, President Leonid Kuchma realized that he could not count on an increasingly independent prime minister with a reputation for integrity, so he replaced. Yushchenko with Viktor Yanukovich.

Viktor Yushchenko's popularity and support remained strong, and in 2004 he ran for election against Viktor Yanukovich for president. The election was aflame with drama as Yanukovich's party applied fraudulent methods to win the campaign, including an attempt to poison Yushchenko. Yushchenko won, however, in a rerun election.

Decades of confrontation between the people and the government in the totalitarian past have created a very suspicious attitude toward law-enforcement bodies. Ukrainians do not trust authorities in general, and remain convinced that involving the police brings more trouble than good. As a result, people try to resolve conflicts among themselves, calling for the police only when there is no other option.

THE MILITARY

A mandatory two-year military service is required of all men in good health, starting at the age of 18. There are some exemptions from military service: those who are an only child supporting elderly parents, those with serious health problems, or those with a family of their own and at least two children born before the father's draft age. College students are sometimes exempted, depending on the political climate in the Verkhovna Rada. Wealthy families or friends of those in positions of authority often "buy" exemptions for their sons. Professional military men and women join the armed forces after graduating from military academies. Volunteers

"Even when good laws were adopted, there was an enormous gap between what the law said and how it was enforced."

—Larisa Afanasyeva, a Russian legal scholar (The New York Times, December 9, 1989)

can apply without special military education. Military service for women is voluntary.

LOCAL GOVERNMENT

The structure of the government is hierarchical, with the federal government at the top of the ladder. Below that are oblasts, districts, each with its own oblast administration, as well as a local version of parliament called the Oblast Council of People's Deputies. Elections to the Oblast Council are held every four years, with each of the elected deputies representing a division within their oblast. The oblast administration is responsible for local governmental affairs, but since its powers are limited, it often only enforces the decisions of the federal government. The head of the oblast administration is the chairman of the Oblast Executive Committee, a position that changes quite often.

Rayon (county) government is a smaller model of the oblast government, but exercises even less autonomy.

A city council represents the interests of residents in cities and towns. The chairperson of the city council, comparable to a mayor, is elected by the population of the city at large. It is the chairperson's duty to assemble an executive committee, members of which are approved or rejected by the city council.

The characteristic feature of local governments and their auxiliary offices is that they are responsible to more than one superior department. An office such as the Department of Agriculture of an oblast (or rayon) is subordinate to the Oblast Council of People's Deputies on one hand and the Ministry of Agriculture on the other, leaving it little room for open decision making. Local authorities endure constant struggles to free themselves from the influence of higher offices. One of the most urgent problems is determining how tax money should be divided among the offices.

After years of living under the one-party system of the Soviet Union, it is not surprising that it was difficult for most Ukrainians to believe that they could actually influence political events. Fortunately, such

The first free election in Ukraine gave Ukrainians an uplifting new sense of power in their ability to change the status quo.

COAT OF ARMS

The coat of arms (Tryzub) features a blue shield with a yellow trident. The history of the trident symbol is more than one thousand years old. The first known archaeological and historical evidence of it has been found on the seals of the Rurik dynasty. The oldest seal is the one of Prince Sviatoslav Ihorevych. Although there is no sure and definite interpretation of the symbol, most historians agree that it probably depicts a stylized hawk or other totem of the first Riurikid rulers' family.

attitudes are gradually changing. Since independence, dozens of new parties reflecting fresh views and political beliefs have arisen to fill the void of the Communist Party. One of the most important and influential parties, Rukh (rookh, movement), was founded by a group of Ukrainian writers in 1989. The Rukh Party started as a political force opposing the Soviet regime and became a vanguard in the movement that led to Ukraine's independence.

Since the advent of free elections in 1993, Ukrainians have grown increasingly confident about their individual power to promote ideas through politics.

FOREIGN RELATIONS

Ukraine's institutional relationship with the EU started when it gained independence in 1991. Ukraine has been the recipient of substantial technical assistance from the EU, largely channeled through the Tacis Program (launched by the EU to support partner countries' initiatives to develop societies based on political freedoms and economic prosperity). In the energy sphere, Ukraine benefited from the EU's Fuel Gap program, aimed to help the country sustain its fuel imports after the last unit of the Chernobyl nuclear plant was closed at the end of 2000.

Despite the positive developments, there are several stumbling blocks hampering relations between Ukraine and the EU. Ukraine has not been officially recognized by the EU as a nation with a market economy. The reasons for that have been the slow progress in economic reforms and the failure to improve Ukraine's human rights record to combat corruption, and to reform the judiciary system. This is particularly disappointing for President Yushchenko, who wants to move decisively toward gaining membership in the European Union.

Ukraine's path toward Europe, however, and away from the Kremlin's traditional sphere of influence, is a major threat to Russia. The political and economic changes in Central and Eastern Europe since 1991 have had extremely adverse effects on Russian trade there. Despite the substantial decline in trade between Russia and Ukraine following the collapse of the Soviet Union, economic interdependence between the two countries is still strong. Russia is Ukraine's biggest importer. In addition, Russia is an important investor in Ukraine, particularly in its oil industry, with four out of the six refineries being owned by Russian companies. Also, ties with Russia are especially strong in the east where many ethnic Russians live. Many of these Ukrainians were born in Russia, have relatives still in Russia, and speak and read primarily in Russian.

In this new era, people are free to criticize the government, although many are still wary of doing so.

ECONOMY

UKRAINE IS ONE OF the richest nations in the world in terms of natural resources. Before independence, Ukraine produced 25 percent of the USSR's industrial output, 25 percent of its agricultural output, 30 percent of its meat, and 50 percent of its iron ore.

An overwhelming majority of Ukraine's people voted for independence not only because they wanted the freedom of cultural expression, but also because they wanted to be masters of their land and resources. Expectations of immediate prosperity, however, soon dissipated, and Ukrainians have been forced to acknowledge the sobering reality of their economic situation. The economy was badly mismanaged by the Soviet state. Despite decades of abuse, the rich black soil that had made Ukraine famous as the breadbasket of Europe still yields abundant harvests. The lack of technology, however, prevents the crops from being processed effectively. In some cases the harvested crops never reach the processing units because the overburdened transportation system is inadequate, particularly when rainy weather turns the roads to mud.

Ukraine's main challenge since independence has been to move away from industrial sectors such as steel, chemicals, machine tooling, shipbuilding, and weaponry. Most of these industries depended heavily on government support and became even less viable when traditional export markets collapsed. The country's attempt at diversifying its products away from these sectors has been gradual, with privatization and foreign investment proceeding more slowly than in other former Soviet countries such as Poland and Hungary.

Above: **The Dnipro hydroelectric plant is one of the largest in Europe. Hydroelectricity is a clean and effective source of energy.**

Opposite: **Lumber waiting to be exported at trade docks in Odessa.**

A state-run steel plant in Kryvyy Rig.

There are massive problems still to be solved by Ukraine. Problems in energy transmissions, poor and inefficient public services, a backward and underdeveloped transportation system, a lack of a "rule of law" in the judicial and law-enforcement systems, and general poverty are just some of the areas that urgently need to be repaired. Widespread corruption, the centralization of decision making in all aspects of Ukrainian society—still existent in private enterprises and in educational, health, governmental, and social institutions—and poor infrastructure form the major contributing factors that impel many Ukrainian professionals to emigrate from Ukraine and seek careers far from home. This costly brain and talent drain further slows the development of a country with great potential. Ukraine's efforts at reform have, moreover, been hampered by its quarrels with Russia about gas distribution and the very socioeconomic problems, political turmoil, and the bottomless scourge of corruption it is trying to subvert.

STATE VERSUS PRIVATE

The best way to praise Ukrainians is to call them a good *khazyayin* (kha-ZIA-yin) for a man or *khazyayka* (kha-ZIAI-ka) for a woman—a good master of the household. This is a reflection of the Ukrainian desire to manage their property as well as possible. The state-run economy discouraged such feelings, which is why early Ukrainian reforms included privatization. Over 9,500 businesses were privatized in early 1995. By 2003, 11,700 small enterprises had been privatized. Large-scale privatization has progressed at a much slower pace, however. A lack of transparency or clear dealings in the privatization process, coupled with virtually no interest among the ruling elites in relinquishing their control over the economic and bureaucratic establishments, have hindered progress in this area.

FAR ABROAD AND NEAR ABROAD

A loose unity of former Soviet states called the Commonwealth of Independent States (CIS) was created in 1992 after the dissolution of the USSR. In that year, Ukraine imported $39 billion worth of products from "near abroad," the term used to describe the countries of the CIS, in comparison with only $5.1 billion from "far abroad," or the rest of the world. It exported $36 billion worth of goods near abroad and $3.6 billion far abroad. Wheat was the main agricultural export product from Ukraine, and the country has become the world's fifth-largest exporter of grains. Its main export commodities are ferrous and nonferrous metals, fuel and petroleum products, chemicals, machinery, transportation equipment, and food products. The industrial sector is dominated by heavy industries— steel (representing 30 percent of the industrial production), coal mining, chemicals, mechanics, and shipbuilding. The country's top three export partners are Russia, Turkey, and Italy. Its top three import partners are Russia, Turkmenistan, and Germany for energy products, hydrocarbons, machinery, and vehicles.

Unable to find jobs in the conventional workforce, many Ukrainians have turned to self-employment. This man is a money changer.

UNEMPLOYMENT

Because of the attempts at transformation to a free-market economy, the level of unemployment in Ukraine increased dramatically. This is explained to some degree by changes in the infrastructure of the industrial and agricultural complex, but it is also very likely because of the greater emphasis put on efficiency—no longer was there any reason to hire two people to do the work of one.

In 2000 Ukraine's official rate of unemployment was 11 percent, but by 2003 unemployment was only reduced to 9.1 percent. In 2006 the country's unemployment rate was an improved 6.7 percent, as calculated by the International Labor Organization. A paradox has occurred between declining unemployment rates and stagnant employment rates. That is partly explained by the slow but steady decrease in the labor force, itself caused somewhat by significant migration abroad during the 1990s. More than 1.2 million individuals emigrated between 1994 and 2003.

There were about 22.5 million employed Ukrainians in 2006. There has been an important shift in employment between the public and private sectors. The years between 1999 and 2003 saw a doubling in private-sector employment, while public employment fell. Despite this, state-owned enterprises remain the largest source of employment.

TRANSPORTATION

The railway system in Ukraine has been developed extensively. There is hardly a town in Ukraine with a population over 10,000 that does not have a railway station, both for freight and passenger trains. Railways dominate the transportation network of the country. In 2005 Ukrainian railways carried 449 million tons of freight and 516 million passengers.

Waterways are also used extensively for transportation needs. Major rivers, such as the Dnipro, the Dnister, and the Pivdennyy Bug, and the Azov and Black seas provide transportation routes for ships and barges year-round. The Black Sea Shipping Company (BLASCO) is one of the largest transportation enterprises in the world.

Airways are not used as widely as they were in the past, although this is changing with growing civilian purchasing power and as business and cultural relations develop. The country's airline, Ukraine International Airlines, together with airlines from 25 foreign countries, maintain regular flights to Ukraine. Most passenger miles are logged between Ukraine and Russia, Germany, the Czech Republic, the United Kingdom, Hungary, Austria, Israel, Turkey, France, Poland, and the Netherlands.

In large cities there are buses and subways. Public transportation is inexpensive and relatively efficient, but during rush hour, passengers can be packed tightly —a familiar experience in New York and Tokyo, too. In remote areas of the country, however, trains may be slower and break down rather frequently.

Commuters arriving at the railway station in Kharkiv.

UKRAINIAN CURRENCY

A temporary "transition period" currency was introduced in 1992, replacing the Russian ruble, the currency used all across the former Soviet Union. The Ukrainian word for the temporary currency was karbovanets (kahr-BOH-vah-nets), though it was often called "coupon." When the coupons were first introduced, there were 1, 3, 5, 10, 25, 50, and 100 karbovanet notes. Later on, because of hyperinflation, these notes became collectors' items. By the first quarter of 1996, the smallest bill was 1,000 and the largest 10,000,000.

The rate of exchange in 1996 was approximately 150,000 karbovanets to the U.S. dollar, so even 10 million karbovanets equaled only $68.

By the third quarter of 1996, the government was finally able to introduce a new Ukrainian currency, called the hryvna, or hryvnia (HRIV-nah). Today the hryvnia is in circulation as a stable medium of exchange in the country and is maintaining a healthy rate of exchange. Many individuals, however, prefer the U.S. dollar or the euro for currency whenever possible.

In the 1930s academician Yevhen Paton introduced the unique technology of whole-welded bridge construction. Several bridges of this kind can be seen on the Dnipro River; many more were built throughout the Soviet Union.

MANUFACTURING

"Made in Ukraine" labels are not commonly seen on products for sale on supermarket shelves in many countries around the world. Ukrainian-made goods exported to foreign markets include jackets, women's apparel, mineral fertilizers, furniture, vodka, and wedding gowns, but many other Ukrainian products have not yet found worldwide consumers. A variety of objects, however, is manufactured for the home market. One of the largest tractor factories is located in Kharkiv, and trucks are produced in Kryvyy Rig. Small cars are made in Zaporizhzhya, buses in Lviv, television sets in Symferopil, Kiev, Smila, and Lviv. Ukraine has a strong base for machine manufacture in a number of industries.

Every year 3,207,000 tons (2,909,000 metric tons) of mineral fertilizers are produced for internal and foreign markets, as well as significant amounts of synthetic fabric, yarn, and polymeric plastics.

Ukraine has the scientific, technical, and industrial basis for the research, development, and production of small arms. Armor equipment is designed and manufactured at three design bureaus and 27 plants. The scientific and industrial potential of Ukraine makes it possible to create and produce modern military communication and automated control systems at two scientific research institutes and 13 plants.

AGRICULTURE

Agricultural land accounts for nearly 70 percent of the total land area in Ukraine, but agriculture accounts for only 24 percent of its gross domestic product. Some 25 percent of the country's labor force works in this industry.

Agricultural success in Ukraine is attributed to its industrious farmers, a moderate climate, and the most fertile black soil in the world—*chornozem* (chor-noh-ZEM). The production of grains and oilseeds is always the main topic with Ukrainian producers and policy makers. Grain covers 56 percent of arable land and is slowly spreading. Oilseeds (mainly sunflower) are grown on 4 percent of the land, and oil crops on about 8 percent of the land. Fodder crops use about 22 percent of the arable land.

The country has become a major grain exporter. Feed winter wheat and feed barley, for animal fodder, are two major export crops. Domestically, Ukraine requires between 5.8 and 6.5 million tons of grain for local consumption. Poultry production has been on the rise since 2000 with heavy investment in the industry.

COLLECTIVE, STATE, AND PRIVATE FARMING

Under the codes of the Soviet state-run economy, private farming was banned. The only exception to the rule were the small, 2-acre (0.8-ha) plots that qualified more as gardens than fields. Collective farms were the norm under the administration of the USSR, with combined ownership

The struggle to privatize farms in Ukraine continues. In 1993, private household plots produced 35 percent of all agricultural products, collective farms, 40 percent, and state farms, 25 percent.

Private land ownership also means ownership of crops grown on the land and the right to sell them in an open market, a new concept for Ukrainians, introducing different social interactions.

of the land and, in theory, collective ownership of everything produced on the land. After independence a growing movement to reintroduce private farming squeezed the government to issue laws that would ensure private land ownership. As a result, family-owned farms have increased significantly in the past decade, becoming a major component of Ukrainian agriculture. In 1990 the share of agricultural land used by house-plot owners and private family farms was only 6 percent. In 2004 this number ballooned to 36 percent.

The size of the average private farm in the past 10 years has increased from 60 to 178 acres (24 to 72 ha). This group of independent farmers relies heavily on the land for both income and subsistence. Most private farms are owned and run by families.

ENERGY

Ukraine consumes about 2.8 trillion cubic feet (80 billion cubic m) of natural gas a year (2005 estimate). About a third of Ukraine's gas is supplied by Russia, while Ukraine produces about 20 percent for its own needs. The remainder comes from Turkmenistan via Russian pipelines.

In 2004 all of Russian gas exports to Europe was funneled through three countries—Ukraine, Belarus, and Moldova—more than 80 percent via Ukraine alone.

Prior to the 2004 presidential elections, the Russian state-owned gas monopoly company, Gazprom, supplied Ukraine with natural gas at the rate of $50 per 1,000 cubic meters (the market rate, in comparison, was $230).

Between 2004 and 2006, a bilateral dispute erupted between Ukraine and Russia over the price of gas. Ukraine did acknowledge the need to pay more for the gas, but believed a sudden sharp increase would

UKRAINE'S GAS CONSUMPTION

Ukraine is one of the most energy-wasteful countries in the world. It consumes more natural gas (80 billion cubic meters in 2005) than Poland, Hungary, the Czech Republic, and Slovakia combined. According to the U.S. Energy Information Administration (IA), the country accounts for 1.5 percent of the world's total energy consumption.

The low cost of gas imported from Russia has had surprisingly negative effects on the country's economy. Heavy industries such as steel and chemical are high users of gas. By keeping the price of gas low (through subsidies by the Ukrainian state company Naftogaz Ukrajiny), the government has been sustaining the existence of these basic industries. As a result, there is less incentive for investors to channel funds from these low value-added industries to information technology or other knowledge-based, future-looking industries.

The impact of the Soviet gas price hike has triggered a sharp rise in the cost to consumers of daily necessities such as public transportation. Almost all Ukrainians depended on virtually free gas for cooking and hot water. Accustomed to having free energy under the Soviets, the transition to more costly utilities has been difficult.

---

severely damage its economy and leave many citizens without heat during the cold winter. This standoff continued until finally, in January 2006, Russia cut off its supply of gas to Ukraine.

Although the action was to impact only the supply to Ukraine, Gazprom's action on European countries dependent on Russian energy was immediate. Several European nations, including Germany and the UK, responded angrily and demanded that Russia resume piping gas. After international pressure, Russia relented and resumed gas flows.

A number of dams have been built on major rivers (the first one, called Dniproges, in 1932). In most cases, however, the end result has been the re-formation of the rivers, leading to devastating floods and massive evacuations.

Coal-burning facilities do not produce great amounts of power and therefore serve limited areas. They are also very harmful to the environment since the by-product is the primary source of acid rain.

There are four operating nuclear power plants currently in Ukraine. Together, these plants account for approximately 24 percent of the country's total power-generating capacity. The last working reactor at the Chernobyl power plant was permanently shut down in December 2000.

ENVIRONMENT

THE NUCLEAR MELTDOWN AT CHERNOBYL in 1986 was probably one of the greatest environmental disasters of the twentieth century. The aftereffect of the damage, especially to the environment, reaches well beyond Chernobyl. In the last two decades of Soviet rule, Soviet industrialization of Ukraine, especially in the Donetsk basin, left a legacy of air pollution and of industrial spill into the Dnieper River, and has contributed to the pollution and decay of the Black Sea.

Surprisingly, economic difficulties in the country have led to some environmental benefits—the shutting down of old and dangerous factories helped reduce carbon emissions. But economic woes and bureaucratic hurdles also severely limited the Ukrainian government's ability to adopt and enforce environmental regulations during this period.

Opposite: **An aeriel view of the Chernobyl nuclear plant in Ukraine after the disaster.**

BLACK SEA AND SEA OF AZOV

The coasts of the Black Sea and the adjoining Sea of Azov make up much of the southern borders of Ukraine. They stretch over five administrative units, or oblasts, and the total length of the coastline is more than 1,865 miles (3,000 km).

The Black Sea and the Sea of Azov are home to nearly 160 species of fish. The Black Sea has fish of Mediterranean origin that make up about 60 percent of the marine population there.

Exhaustive economic development over the last decade has resulted in considerable ecological pressure and imbalance to the area. This has led to great changes in the natural conditions of the seas, causing pollution.

One of the negative effects is seashore erosion caused by dredging and hydromechanical works conducted in the territorial waters and on the Black Sea shelf. Around 245 acres (100 ha) of land is washed away annually. This causes territories to shrink, hindering town planning and tourism development, and negatively affecting the coastline's ecological system. The few measures to protect the seashore are fragmented and do not constitute a joint protection system along the entire Ukrainian coastline. Following the adoption of several governmental regulations, about 95 miles (150 km) of the shore has been reinforced.

AIR POLLUTION

Since independence, Ukraine has encouraged the formation of numerous environmental organizations, and as a result, there is general awareness among the people of the harmful effects of air pollution. Grave environmental

Mixed urban development along the Black Sea coast in Ukraine.

damages of the Soviet past have come to light and have been replaced by more environmentally friendly legislation, regulation, and practice.

As in most other countries, however, the main source of pollution in large cities is road traffic. The chemical industry also adds to air pollution, and oil refineries pollute underground waters. No substantial progress has been achieved in pollution control by the machine-making industry. Although its share in the total emissions of pollutants is relatively small, the specific contaminants present are much more hazardous to health than in other industries.

In 2005 the government imposed regulations to protect children against indoor and outdoor air pollution, such as the prohibition of using certain building materials for children's institutions. A special problem that was addressed is the air quality in Internet cafés, which are often open 24 hours and heavily used by younger people. Research found that formaldehyde levels in the cafés were 20 times over the limit, that pollution from heavy metals was present, and that there were strong electromagnetic fields caused by the proximity of so many computers in enclosed spaces.

Dense smoke rising from a power station's chimney as a prolonged cold grips the capital of Kiev in January 2006, with temperatures descending to -22°F (-30°C) in some parts of the country.

WILDLIFE

Over 40,000 species of animals live in Ukraine, including the water areas of the Black Sea and the Sea of Azov. Vertebrates include fish (about 170 species), amphibians (17 species), reptiles (21 species), birds (over 400 species), and mammals (about 110 species).

Ukraine nests more than 100 species out of the 170 species of birds listed in the Agreement on the Conservation of African-Eurasian Migratory Waterbirds. Some of the endangered species of birds in Ukraine include the black stork, black and Griffon vultures, osprey, and golden eagle. The wetlands of southern Ukraine, such as Syvash, are places of particular importance as they are home to hundreds of thousands of birds.

Ukraine is particularly attentive to the protection, rehabilitation, and use of wild animals (mainly vertebrates) because of their vulnerability and industrial value. The Red Data Book of Ukraine, an official list of rare and endangered species of animals, plants, and fungi, names those prohibited from illegal catching and disbursement, and identifies protected natural areas of great importance for the animals.

WATER USE AND MANAGEMENT

The government of Ukraine is now focusing on increasing the accessibility to clean drinking water. The lack of this poses significant health and environmental concerns to the Ukrainian populace. Although nearly the entire population has access to safe drinking water, the current network is overexploited. As a result of the rising population pressure on the limited supply of potable water, many cities receive water only twice a day for a limited number of hours. Tourists are advised not to drink tap water, and many Ukrainians drink bottled water or water from wells in rural areas.

The country's main water basins are the Dnieper, the Dniester, the Danube, the Siversky Donetsk, and the Southern Bug. All these basins drain south toward the Black Sea and the Sea of Azov. The Dnieper, the major river, is fed by several tributaries and divides the country into two parts. Six large reservoirs built on the river provide water for the industrial centers of Donbas, for irrigation in Crimea and the Black Sea coast, and for hydropower generation. About 60 percent of the population depends on the Dnieper for its drinking-water supply.

In 1999, apart from the rivers in Crimea, all river basins in Ukraine were classified either as polluted or very polluted. Most of the pollution came from agricultural activity. Mining and industrial activities have also contributed to the pollution, although the volume of effluence has declined as a result of the industrial recession. Untreated industrial and animal wastes, indiscriminate discharges of toxic sewage, excessive fertilization, and runoff from areas hit by the Chernobyl incident are some of the pollutants that render many of Ukraine's water resources unsafe for consumption even today.

Opposite: **Storks play in their nest in the abandoned village of Kozhushki in the Chernobyl region.**

Opposite (inset): **Sparrows perched in a frozen bush near Chernobyl.**

Below: **A canal linking Ukraine's ecologically sensitive Danube River Delta to the Black Sea in the southern Odessa region.**

Ukraine's basic legislation for water resources are the 1991 Law on Environmental Protection and the 1995 Water Code. There are plans to review its environmental legislation, and the long-range plan is to integrate its laws with those of the European Union's environmental directives. In 1999 a survey conducted by the United Nations Development Program (UNDP) revealed that less than 65 percent of those surveyed had running water in their homes. The UNDP has taken initiatives to reform water supply systems in Ukraine's rural areas.

THE CHERNOBYL DISASTER—20 YEARS ON

On April 26, 1986, the fourth reactor at the Chernobyl nuclear power plant exploded, causing the radioactive contamination of huge territories surrounding the site. About 9 tons of nuclear-reactive materials were discharged into the air. The disaster released at least 100 times more radiation than the atomic bombs dropped on Nagasaki and Hiroshima. Much of the contamination was deposited close to Chernobyl, in parts of Belarus, Ukraine, and Russia. After the incident, however, traces of radioactive deposits were found in nearly every country in the northern hemisphere. Wind currents and uneven rainfall left some areas more heavily contaminated than their immediate neighbors.

The number of deaths caused by the accident remains highly controversial. The UN-led Chernobyl Forum estimated that there will yet be a number of deaths from illnesses such as cancer, but said that most people's problems are economic and psychological, not medical or environmental.

Once the reactor fires had been extinguished, a sarcophagus encasing was constructed by the Soviets to entomb the fourth reactor. The encasing was built in haste, however, and is now crumbling. Despite reinforcing, there are fears it could collapse and release tons more of radioactive dust. Work has begun on a replacement shelter, designed to last 100 years, and it may be completed by 2008. The new shelter will stand as tall as the Statue of Liberty and will be slipped over the sarcophagus like a hood.

In spite of the lasting contamination of the area, wildlife is showing a dramatic revival. Scientists have recorded the presence of a thriving population of wild horses, boars, and wolves. Lynx have returned to the area, and birds have nested right in the reactor without any obvious ill effects.

UKRAINIANS

DESPITE INVASION AND OCCUPATION by foreign conquerors and the number of minorities living in the country, Ukrainians have retained their predominantly Slavic physical features. Quite a remarkable number of Ukrainians can also be found throughout the world. Emigrants have had several reasons for leaving home—escaping political oppression, cruel landlords, and unbearable economic hardships.

Massive emigration from Ukraine occurred at the beginning of the 20th century when continuous turmoil in Russia caused many people to search for better living conditions abroad. After the Communists took over in Ukraine, there were a number of dissidents who preferred (or were forced) to live abroad rather than submit to Communist rule. The largest number of Ukrainians abroad live in Canada, followed by the United States.

Despite the large numbers of people who have emigrated from Ukraine, it is still one of the most densely populated countries in Europe. Ukraine has a population of 46.6 million, 68 percent of whom live in urban areas. The majority identify themselves as Ukrainians (78 percent). The second largest group is Russian (17 percent). The remaining 5 percent include Byelorussians, Moldavians, Bulgarians, Crimean Tatars, Jews, and Roma, or Gypsies.

Above: **This little flower girl is one of the large group of Russians living in Ukraine.**

Opposite: **Traditional Ukrainian costume highlights a festival day for this young woman.**

MINORITIES

Ethnically, Ukraine is a fairly homogeneous society. Nonetheless, there are small groups of people living in the central and southwestern areas who differ from the mainstream Ukrainians, although they are related ethnically. Until 1946 the Lemky lived throughout the Carpathian Mountains on both the eastern and western sides. Now they are confined to a small area in the westernmost part of Ukraine. Only recently the Lemky exchanged their traditional dress, called *chuby* (CHOO-hee, a woolen covering without sleeves), for modern clothes.

The Boiky are mountaineers who live slightly farther east than the Lemky. Their main occupation is cattle breeding. The Boiky have maintained many of their ancient customs, particularly in architecture. The area they inhabit is spotted with old-style churches and wooden houses with large entrance halls. Even today it is not uncommon to see a Boiky man or woman—dressed in a traditional long cloak decorated with beads—tilling the soil using traditional agricultural tools.

The Volhynians inhabit the northern mountain areas. They are known for their musical talents, especially lyre playing and singing. Their festive carols and religious songs have been particularly well preserved.

The most notable of the ethnic minorities are the Hutsuls, who breed cattle and sheep and are heavily engaged in forestry. They are known throughout Ukraine for their exceptional craftsmanship and building

A Hutsul man in the Carpathian Mountains leads his cow from pasture.

techniques. Wood carving, pottery making, brass work, and rug weaving are among the highly developed Hutsul crafts. For hundreds of years, the Hutsuls have carved objects made of wood, such as doors, chests, and crosses, with intricate geometric patterns and beaded inlays. Today their handicrafts are sold throughout Ukraine, some commanding very high prices.

A makeshift cabin atop the Carpathian Mountains is used by a Hutsul family when they move their cattle to pasture.

This young Tatar boy is copying from the Koran. The Tatars were converted to Islam in the 14th century, and as Sunnites, were instrumental in bringing Islam to Turkistan. Many Tatars, however, have clung to their pre-Islamic beliefs in spirits that inhabit the forests, the water, and the household.

THE TATARS

The Turkic peoples can be divided into two main groups, eastern and western. The eastern Turks, which includes people living in Turkey and regions of the former Soviet Union, including Crimea, are sometimes characterized as dark-skinned, but many are as fair as western Europeans.

The western Turks, called Tatars, consist of two groups—those living in the former Tatar Autonomous Soviet Socialist Republic (ASSR), located in the middle of the Volga River basin, and those inhabiting the Crimean Peninsula. The peninsula was incorporated into the Crimean ASSR in 1921 and continued to be populated primarily by Tatars. In 1944 the republic was abolished and the Tatars were deported to Siberia and Central Asia for allegedly collaborating with the Nazis.

Although their homeland was officially rehabilitated in 1967, the Crimean Tatars were not permitted to return to it, and only now, after the dissolution of the Soviet Union, are they beginning to trickle back.

The Tatars are well known as traders, but they also have an ancient tradition of craftsmanship in wood, ceramics, leather, cloth, and metal. During the 9th to the 15th centuries, the Tatar economy became based on a combination of farming and herding that continues to this day. As a medieval power, the Tatars had a complex social organization with distinct classes. At the head of the government stood the khan.

NATIONAL FEATURES

The expression *schyryy ukrayinets* (SHCHIH-riy ook-rah-YI-nets), meaning "sheer Ukrainian," is more a reflection of the dominant features of the unique Ukrainian character than of physical features.

A typical Ukrainian may have dark or blond hair, and gray, blue, or brown eyes, and as a people their personalities may be just as diverse. But one thing that all Ukrainians are taught from the time they are young is hospitality.

When there is a guest in the house, whether staying for several hours or several days, the host's personal life is sacrificed almost completely. In extreme cases, many Ukrainians will take leave from their jobs and provide the guest with the best possible accommodation, even if it means temporarily giving up their bedrooms.

Feeding a guest is also part of Ukrainian hospitality, and no expense is spared to ensure that the meal is well prepared and the guest well fed. Children are taught at a young age that providing a good meal for a guest is the most important obligation in hospitality. As a result, many visitors have left Ukraine with the mistaken impression that Ukrainians eat like royalty every night of the week.

A Ukrainian woman with blond hair and gray eyes displays the beautiful embroidery created in her homeland.

Typical Ukrainian festival dress is colorful and intricately designed.

NATIONAL DRESS

Traditional national dress for both women and men is characterized by intricate embroidery with distinct variations in style, depending on the district of Ukraine it comes from. Nowadays, the Ukrainian national dress is worn only at folk festivals.

Men's dress is simpler than that of women, consisting of very loose trousers, pulled tight at the waist by a sash and at the ankles by laces, and a flaxen (linen) shirt with long sleeves. Depending on the season, men may also wear an overcoat with long, wide sleeves, and a hat that looks something like a stocking cap. Boots are made of leather and worn to the knee. All the garments are worn loose to allow for ease in movement. This is because Ukrainian national dress dates back to the time of the Kozaks when clothing had to be loose and suitable for fighting.

In earlier times, it was easy to distinguish between a married and an unmarried woman, since Orthodox Church rules obliged a married woman to cover her hair with a kerchief. Unmarried women, on the other hand, wore colorful ribbons in their hair as decorations. Coral beads were worn around the neck as part of the outfit, and since a string of such beads was sometimes equal to the value of a cow, the number of strands a woman wore was an indicator of her family's wealth.

When performing Ukrainian folk dances, women now wear a unique style of dress traditional to their part of the country. A brightly colored woolen skirt is worn over a petticoat and covered with a white apron. An embroidered white blouse with a vest is worn as a top. On their heads, women wear a floral headdress with streamers flowing down the back.

In western Ukraine, there are some significant differences in national dress. This is explained by the influence of neighboring Hungary, Poland, and Romania. Thus, at folk festivals, men wear tight pants, sometimes vests, and tight overcoats. Their hats are round, with moderately wide rims, and decorated with rooster's feathers. The women have distinctive headpieces and wear skirts tied at the waist and sometimes open at the front to reveal another embroidered layer.

Today women dress comfortably, though usually in dresses, to work in the fields during the hot summer days. Married women still wear the traditional kerchief on their heads.

SENSE OF HUMOR

According to some observers, hard times can lead people to develop a sense of humor. In the old days, when things got rough, people laughed at themselves and each other to diminish the pain of misfortune, for laughter was one good thing that was affordable for everyone.

If this is the case, it is easy to understand why Ukrainians have a very keen sense of humor. Ukrainian humor deals with a variety of situations, from laughing at oneself to satirizing the government (until recently, considered very risky business). The ability to tell jokes well is highly admired by Ukrainians.

The city of Odessa has always been the center of comedy, not only for Ukraine, but for the former USSR as well. Regardless of governmental restrictions, humor festivals were held annually on April 1 in Odessa—April Fools' Day. Since independence, these festivals have become huge events that attract thousands of smiling visitors each year.

UKRAINIAN NAMES

Ukrainian names are partially of Slavic origin, partially of biblical origin, sometimes borrowed from Greece (because of the Byzantine influence), and, recently, adopted from other European nations.

Names of Slavic origin date to pagan times and usually reflect the qualities for which men and women were admired in those days. For example, Svitlana, meaning full of light; Liudmyla, loved by people; Volodymyr, world owner; and Myroslav, praised by the community, are all popular Slavic names.

Sometimes Ukrainian spelling and pronunciation disguises the relation of Ukrainian names to the same names in English. For example, John in English is Ivan in Ukrainian, and Mary is Mariya.

Ukrainian last names are derived from male ancestors' names. Of course, it is difficult to find a family who can trace its family name all the way back to the originator, but it is possible to presume that Ivanchuk clearly had a male ancestor named Ivan. Other names, such as Kovalchuk, an exact equivalent of the name Smith, were derived from professional skills.

Ukrainians do not have middle names. Instead, they use patronymic names, which are formed by adding a suffix to the name of the person's father. For example, the patronymic of a woman whose father's name is Ivan, is Ivanivna, and her brother's patronymic is Ivanovych. When meeting someone for the first time in Ukraine, it is polite to call them by their first and patronymic names, rather than using only the first name or last name. For example, "I'm happy to meet you, Mariya Ivanivna."

HOW UKRAINIANS ARE CHARACTERIZED

Throughout the Soviet Union, Ukrainians were often thought of as provincial, particularly by Russians. Some Russians still refer to Ukrainian men as home-bound farmers, who save as much as can be saved and are too thrifty to have fun. Correspondingly, Ukrainian women are sometimes thought of as simple housewives who are not interested in events outside the home, a stereotype of mythical proportions considering the majority of women in Ukraine work outside the home.

People living in eastern Ukraine are believed to be involved almost exclusively in the mining industry, and to drink more alcohol than other Ukrainians. The population of the city of Odessa is considered to be very entrepreneurial and lazy, but with a superior sense of humor. People in western Ukraine are famous for their conservatism, hard-working character, and ultranationalism.

Svetlana Savitskaya is a modern Ukrainian who has made a name for herself internationally as a cosmonaut.

FAMOUS UKRAINIANS

Ukraine's history as a satellite state under the Soviet Union, and then Russia, made it difficult for prominent Ukrainians to be recognized. Those who did become famous were almost always directly connected with Ukraine's struggle for independence. Lesya Ukrayinka (1871–1913) took her last name from her beloved country. Many of this poet's works were dedicated to the movement for liberation, as well as expressions of love for her mother and for the motherland itself.

Two prominent leaders in the 17th century, Hetman Bohdan Khmelnytskyy (1595–1657) and Hetman Ivan Mazepa (1639–1709), were each involved in attempts to liberate Ukraine. Khmelnytskyy entered into a union with Russia to eliminate ongoing threats from Poland. Mazepa tried to liberate Ukraine from Russia by forming an alliance with Charles XII of Sweden. These two names are found in every Ukrainian history book.

In the city of Smila (which means brave), there is a legend of a brave young girl who sacrificed her life to warn Ukrainian defenders of approaching Mongol troops. In Kam'yanets-Podilskyy, a tragic and beautiful legend describes the story of 400 girls who tied their braids together and leaped down from the walls of the fortress to avoid being enslaved.

TARAS HRYHOROVYCH SHEVCHENKO (1814–61)

Two books are in nearly every household in Ukraine: the Bible and *Kobzar* (*The Bard*) by Taras Shevchenko. Shevchenko was born into a family of peasants in central Ukraine. From his early childhood he showed signs of genius. His love for his people and his enormous talent (he was a poet, a painter, and an engraver) changed the son of illiterate serfs into the enlightened prophet of the Ukrainian people, a creator of the Ukrainian literary language, and an inspiration for generations of Ukrainian independence fighters. Monuments to Shevchenko stand in nearly every town and in any place in the world where there is a significant population of Ukrainians. There is a beautiful monument in Washington, D.C., erected by Ukrainian Americans acknowledging the poet's achievements.

*And in the great new family,
The family of the free,
With softly spoken, kindly word
Remember also me*

—From Shevchenko's Testament, addressed to the world in the hope that one day the world's family would be free

LIFESTYLE

UKRAINE HAS AN ANCIENT AGRICULTURAL heritage, but the majority of its population is urban. In recent years, migration to urban centers has caused tremendous population growth in the cities. This urban movement is usually perpetuated by the desire for a higher standard of living. In the city, one can enjoy concerts, movies, shopping centers, restaurants, a developed system of public transportation, central heating, direct long-distance telephone dialing, and cable television. In the country, there are no concert halls, few movie theaters, no public transportation, no cable television (and television in general is limited to one or two channels), no central heating (which means in many cases using coal and wood stoves all winter long), and no telephones, or, for the few people who have them, limited options for long-distance calling.

Above: **A plain and sturdy rural house in western Ukraine.**

Opposite: **This woman, tending her farm in the Carpathian Mountains, typifies Ukranians who continue to work hard until late in life.**

In the country, the roads are dry and dusty in the summer, wet and muddy in the autumn and spring, and deep in snow and ice in the winter. Shopping is confined to one or two small "products" stores (the equivalent of grocery stores). Since few people own cars, trips to a city are rare and tiring. Bus schedules are unreliable and fares are costly.

The cities provide a wide range of educational options. There are no colleges in rural areas, which means in order to pursue a career other than farming or mining, Ukrainians must travel to the city to study. Taking everything into consideration, many people sacrifice the advantages of rural life—fresh air, natural food, low crime rates, and a quiet pace of life—for a more hectic but more convenient lifestyle in the cities.

A street of old apartment buildings in Lviv.

A HOUSE OR AN APARTMENT?

Ukrainians live in private houses on farms and in small towns. Although this may seem like a luxury to some, Ukrainians who live in houses do not necessarily do so by choice. There are few apartment buildings other than those in large cities. With the recent growth in urban areas, inadequate housing has become a problem. Because the socialist order claimed to provide free services to its citizens, theoretically housing was free for everyone. Registering with a city administration was all any citizen needed to do to be assigned a place to live.

Of course, the standards were very low and many families shared one kitchen, but some apartments had the advantage of a few modern conveniences, such as indoor bathrooms and central heating. Apartments like these were owned by the city, so the rent was insignificant and the utilities were very cheap. The catch was to acquire the apartment as soon as possible after someone vacated, because in some cases the waiting list consisted of a thousand names. In these cases a family had to live with parents or rent an apartment from private owners, which could cost up to 25 percent of their monthly income for ten years or more, while waiting.

Private ownership was discouraged since construction and repair materials were either in short supply or unbearably expensive, and services were difficult to obtain. Even if building a house were an option, people preferred to live in an apartment where they were responsible only for maintaining the interior.

After independence, occupants had the option to buy or sell apartments in which they had been living. Many families could not afford the upkeep of larger apartments because utilities became very expensive, so they had to sell their apartments and buy smaller ones. For some, the living conditions were worse but just the knowledge of owning their own home was enough.

DERYBASIVSKA STREET

Derybasivska Street is the main thoroughfare in downtown Odessa, the port city on the Black Sea. The street has an unusual history. After the Russian Revolution of 1917, street names were changed to honor Soviet functionaries. In 1920 Derybasivska Street, named to commemorate one of Odessa's honorary citizens, General DeRibas, was renamed Lassalya Street, in honor of one of the Russian revolutionaries. Plates with the new name replaced old ones on the walls of the houses along the street. But by morning the plates had disappeared, and chalk and paint had been used to inscribe the old name. Numerous attempts to mount the new plates on the street failed, and finally the Soviet authorities gave up. Thus Derybasivska Street kept its name throughout the decades, much to the pride of the city's residents.

Soviet state policy transformed the suburbs of large cities into giant housing complexes. Today, apartment buildings of between 5 and 16 stories still stretch for miles. Ukrainians call the buildings "ant colonies." More and more people prefer the idea of owning private houses. Unfortunately for the overwhelming majority, a decent house in the city is still not affordable, and costly improvements to these shoddy high-rise apartments have yet to be made.

BACKYARD FARMING

Under the Communist regime, wages earned from working on a collective farm very rarely met the needs of the average Ukrainian family, and while members of a collective farm enjoyed discount prices for products produced on-site, there was rarely enough cash to spare for anything but other kinds of food. The solution for many families was to plant vegetables in a small plot of land near their house, a kind of extended backyard with a few fruit trees, a cow or two in a small barn, several chickens, and three or four pigs. This type of private farming helped collective farmers to extend their food choices and to support their families, because any surplus could be sold at the farmers' market in the nearest town.

Even those living in small towns in private houses began using their backyards for raising fresh vegetables, eggs, and meat for their tables—and sometimes a little cash.

Resting a moment after making a haystack in the backyard.

UKRAINIAN WOMEN

Gender-based discrimination is against the law, but Ukraine still has a long way to go before the sexes are truly equal. A woman in Ukraine would be lucky indeed if her husband helped her in the kitchen, to say nothing of his ever taking complete charge of cleaning the house and running other errands, like shopping for food—an exhausting daily obligation. Instead, the principle that "he brings home the money, she runs the home" is widely practiced. The irony of this is that Ukraine's economy makes it impossible for a man to earn enough to support his entire family, which means that wives must bear a double load.

Women in executive business positions are rare, and the percentage of women in parliament is insignificant. The situation is slightly better at the oblast and city levels of administration. Traditional nurturing occupations are still the most common professions for women: preschool teachers, pediatricians, and cooks.

Although Ukraine remains in many aspects a traditional society in its treatment of women, in recent years several laws have been enacted by the Ukrainian government to broaden women's rights. The Ukrainian parliament allows women to take maternity leave from their jobs for up to three years. During this period, a mother receives a small sum of money from the state each month, called "milk money," in place of her salary. After the leave, the woman may return to her position in the company for which she had worked.

A mother can receive sick leave from work to stay home with an ill child. By law, a father can do this also, although in practice it very rarely happens, since the mother is usually responsible for such homely duties.

FAMILY LIFE

In the last 30 years, the average family size in Ukraine has declined from five members to three. This is because many couples postpone having children until they own a place of their own. Since housing costs are exorbitant, most young couples continue to live with their parents for some years.

In some cities, community centers are run by churches to give older children a place to go after school.

Despite this decline, the birth of a child is a most joyous occasion. If finances allow, Ukrainians prefer that the new mother stay at home for as long as possible. In many cases, though, a mother must return to work, particularly if a long break jeopardizes her career. In these cases the family must search elsewhere for child care. Since it is still common for three generations to live under the same roof, the responsibility of looking after the children often falls on the grandparents. If the grandparents do not live with their children, parents can turn to the well-developed network of child-care centers.

In Ukraine babies can be accepted at child-care centers when they are only 11 months old, but most parents, unless it is absolutely necessary, prefer to delay using these centers until the child has reached 2 or 3 years of age.

Unlike in many other countries, Ukrainian adult children are legally obliged to support their elderly or disabled parents. Of course, it is a moral obligation that children are taught when they are young and that they see everywhere, so legal action is rare. Retirement facilities in Ukraine are exclusively state-run, and for the most part, conditions in such facilities are bleak.

EDUCATION

Twelve years of schooling are mandatory in Ukraine. Schools are state-run, and any deviation from the standard curriculum, established by the Ministry of Education, is discouraged. The objective of general schooling is to give younger students a good knowledge of the

A university in Lviv. Only 20 percent of Ukrainian students manage to enter higher educational institutions because the competition for colleges is fierce with as many as 20 applicants for each opening.

fundamentals of the arts and sciences and to teach them how to use this knowledge practically.

Children start first grade at the age of 6. Primary education takes four years to complete, middle school takes five, and then there are three years of high school to undergo. Ukraine's Law on Education states that provision of elementary schools must be made wherever there are students. Grades 10 to 12 are secondary school levels.

After the ninth grade, Ukrainian students used to have the option of going to a vocational or technical school rather than completing their secondary school education. Vocational and technical school programs could last anywhere from one year (if entered after graduation from secondary school) to three years (if entered after the ninth grade). Today, however, secondary education is compulsory. While in the 12th grade, students sit for the school-leaving examinations or the Government Tests, which also serve as tests for university admission. Getting into a college or university is very competitive. Applicants are required to produce a secondary school certificate and to pass four entrance examinations. The academic year begins in September and ends in July and consists of two academic semesters. There are more than 300 universities and academies in Ukraine, and some 200 are state-run.

Because the state does not have the resources to supply them, staples such as pain relievers and disposable syringes are often not available in hospitals.

The life expectancy for the generation of Ukrainians born in 1993 or 1994 is 68 years. Men live on the average for 62 years, and women for 74 years. These expectations are among the lowest in Europe. The reasons in part are the difficult living conditions, stress, alcoholism, poor health care, and a polluted environment, including significant radioactive contamination from the Chernobyl reactor disaster of 1986.

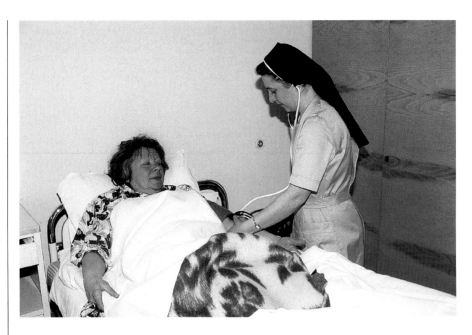

HEALTH CARE

Providing health care for the population is one of the key functions of the state as set out in the Ukrainian Constitution of 1996. State health care is provided under three categories: national, regional, and district levels. The vast majority of health-care services are provided by publicly owned facilities. Private medical clinics are available as well. Their charges are the most expensive, but the level of such care is considered better.

Working as a medical doctor in Ukraine is not as lucrative as it is in many countries, therefore many patients try to ensure that doctors take a personal interest in their case by offering them gifts and money in return for what they feel to be better treatment. In fact, this has almost become the rule. Most hospitals lack essential medicines and equipment, so experienced patients get their doctor's advice ahead of time and arrive at the hospital with their own supplies.

The role of voluntary health insurance is relatively small. Although over 100 private companies offer health insurance, altogether they cover only about 2 percent of the population. This scant coverage is largely because of the high cost of commercial insurance premiums, which are unaffordable for most of the people.

SOCIAL SERVICES

The official retirement age in Ukraine is 55 for women and 60 for men. Pensions are based on years of employment and salary averages during the final two years of service. The amount of the pension is rarely more than 50 percent of the salary.

Since independence, inflation, unstable prices, and general shortages have caused most retired people to seek part-time jobs in order to survive. There are no private retirement homes, not only because the concept itself is culturally unusual and very new, but also because the overwhelming majority of retirees would not be able to afford the charges. State-run facilities are free, but they are used only as a last resort, since the abysmal conditions there are usually close to unbearable.

In addition to retirement homes, there are state-run orphanages and homes for the disabled, kept running mostly by the devotion of the staff and, more recently, by donations from newly created private businesses.

Scant state funds barely cover even the most basic of necessities for establishments such as this one for disabled children.

75

COMMUNICATIONS

"It is better to see once than to hear 100 times." This proverb characterizes the Ukrainian attitude toward communication. Ukrainians do not place a great deal of trust in telephones, faxes, or letters, therefore personal contact is always preferred. Meetings can be for a variety of purposes, either for business, entertainment, or just to relax with friends.

Serious matters are never discussed over the telephone, not only because a Ukrainian prefers to discuss important issues in person but also because telephone communication is unreliable and poorly developed. Ukraine has seen a steady increase in the number of mobile phone users, however, which totaled 17.3 million by 2005.

Local calls rarely present a problem, but long-distance calls are usually a challenge. Not only is it difficult to get through to the desired party but the quality of the connection is often poor, and the line may be disconnected at any moment without warning. Telephones are not a fixed commodity in every household. Less than 50 percent of families have a phone in their homes. It is very difficult to have a telephone installed, since terminals are in short supply. More sophisticated methods of communication, like fax machines, are found mostly in businesses. Electronic mail is slowly increasing with the growth in Internet users. Regular mail is more popular, but it is not absolutely reliable.

EMPLOYMENT

According to the existing constitution, every Ukrainian citizen has the right to be employed. This fundamental right was protected by the USSR as well.

The transition from a state-run to a market economy has not been as smooth as many once envisioned. New private businesses open and close almost weekly. Only a fraction of one percent of newly registered private companies survive. Entrepreneurs expect that their independent businesses will produce immediate financial rewards, but most of them do not have the skills, knowledge, or persistence to lead their companies to success.

Unemployment rates are rising and now officially hover between 5 to 10 percent. In 2006 it was recorded as 6.7 percent by the International Labor Organization, although the official figure given by the government was 2.7 percent. Interestingly, Ukraine has a high rate of female employees (64 percent compared with 73 percent for men). Despite similar educational levels, women nonetheless tend to have lower-paying jobs, and there are somewhat more poor female-headed households than poor male-headed households.

State-run stores like this one are rapidly becoming a thing of the past. Most Ukrainians have been forced to find new jobs since the conversion to privately run shops and factories has eliminated the settings for over-staffing.

MOVING AROUND

"A car is not a luxury, but a means of transportation." This Soviet slogan never became a reality. Even today, cars are used mostly for special trips. Only 1 family out of 10 in Ukraine owns a car. Cars, even those made in the former Soviet Union, were always extremely expensive. In the 1980s, for example, with an average family income of around 4,500 rubles per year, a small popular car called a Zhyguli (zhih-goo-LIH) costs between 8,000 to 12,000 rubles. Domestic cars were often not available for purchase, and foreign models were totally banned from the market.

The situation is approximately the same today. The market has slowly been opened to foreign cars, however, and today it is common to see used foreign cars on Ukrainian streets.

In Soviet Ukraine, gasoline and car repairs were very cheap. Today, most Ukrainians cannot afford to buy a car, or even maintain one they already own, although city streets are surprisingly crowded at times.

The only thing never in short supply were parking spaces, available rather easily even in large city centers. Parking is increasingly a problem in Kiev, however, and cars can be found parked illegally on sidewalks and planted areas.

With some effort one can get tickets for passenger trains that run throughout Ukraine. There is usually a shortage of seats, however, particularly at holiday times when many people are traveling.

Buses also travel to different cities in Ukraine, but the poor condition of the roads means that trips are long and uncomfortable. Most Ukrainians travel by bus only when train tickets are not available. Airplane travel to international destinations is still only a dream for most Ukrainians.

PUBLIC TRANSPORTATION

All of the different kinds of public transportation in Ukraine are easily affordable to the average citizen. The most common forms in most cities are buses, trolleybuses, and trams—typically old and worn-out. In cities with

populations over one million, there is usually a subway. The subway, though as crowded as any other public transportation system in Ukraine, is efficient and runs on time. Electric trains take people from the suburbs and neighboring towns to the city's central railway station. For those who can afford them, there are taxis, but in Kiev during peak traffic hours it is usually faster to ride the subway than to take a taxi.

RELIGION

ORTHODOX CHRISTIANITY is the dominant religion throughout Ukraine, with over 35 million Ukrainians belonging to the Orthodox Church. When Ukraine fell to the Russians in the 17th century, the Ukrainian Orthodox Church was absorbed into the Russian Orthodox Church. Only since 1990 have Ukrainians been able to worship in their own language once more.

Other than slight differences in the procedures of the service, the two churches are nearly identical. Services are held in churches and cathedrals, although it is not easy to find an active church in Ukraine, since so many of them were converted to museums during the years of Soviet domination. Religious education, once limited to Kiev and Odessa seminaries, is regaining popularity. The Orthodox Church is so influential that its representatives can be found in parliament, local legislatures, electoral campaigns, and even in the army.

Above: **Building a new wooden church in Verchovyna.**

Opposite: **Golden domes of the Ukrainian Orthodox Church in Odessa.**

CHRISTIANITY IN UKRAINE

Pre-Christian Ukrainians (the people of Kievan Rus) were pagans. Their beliefs were centered around the powers of nature, and gods were representations of nature's various elements: wind, rain, frost, and so forth. In a country with long, cold winters, the god of the sun was the most powerful. If appropriately worshipped, the gods had the ability to bestow fertility, sunshine, wealth, and health. When defied, however, the gods sent drought, disease, and war. Reflections of some pagan beliefs can still be found in many Christian traditions.

An image of Saturn, the god of agriculture. The Roman festival of Saturn, Saturnalia, is still celebrated in much of the Western world.

Christianity made its way to Kievan Rus almost immediately after the state was formed, in the seventh century. Small groups of the population exposed to the influences of the Byzantine Empire adopted Christianity in the eighth and ninth centuries. The presence of Christian military men from Constantinople in 860 hastened the spread of the religion, adding to the number of believers.

Only a century later, in 988, Prince Volodymyr the Great adopted Christianity as the official religion for Kievan Rus. His decision was dictated by the growing popularity of Christianity in Europe, and the need to integrate Kievan Rus into the cultural, political, and economic life of the West. It was the Greek branch of Christianity that prevailed and became the model on which Ukrainian and Russian Christianity were based for centuries to come.

Nonetheless, the transition from pagan to Christian beliefs was not a smooth one. Russian chronicles tell of a crowd of Kiev's inhabitants driven forcibly by soldiers to the Dnipro River and baptized there en masse. Statues of pagan gods were dismantled, burned, or thrown into the Dnipro. Many names in modern Kiev reflect the events of those days. For example, the main street in Kiev is Hreschatyk (hreh-SCHAH-tik), a derivation of "to cross," or "to baptize," because it was the route by which the pagan crowd was herded to the river. Another part of the city is called Holosiyivka (hoh-loh-SIH-iv-kah), from the Ukrainian "to weep," because it was there that those who managed to escape from the forced baptism grieved for their banished gods.

CHRISTIAN ARCHITECTURE

Constantinople sent missionaries to help Kievan Rus establish Christianity. Byzantine priests taught Kievan volunteers, who became the first Kievan priests. Byzantine architects taught Kievan master builders to erect Christian churches, which is when the beautiful onion-domed cathedrals first appeared in Kiev, Novgorod, Volodymyr, and many other cities of Kievan Rus. The first cathedrals were needed as soon as possible, so they were built of wood and covered with shingles. The typical feature in all Orthodox churches, ancient and modern, is the tripartite construction: a vestibule (or entrance hall) located in the west, a sanctuary in the east (the sanctuary is the part of the church where only the priest and his assistants are admitted), and the main congregational area in between. The tradition of building bell towers separately from the churches originated so as not to overload the wooden structures. As architecture became more sophisticated, brick and stone churches were built often with several chapels surrounding the central room. A church was always constructed in the form of a cross, no matter how many parts it consisted of. Unlike many other churches, Ukrainian Orthodox churches do not have any pews, and those who come to worship either stand or kneel on the hard floor during services.

An old Orthodox church made of wood and covered in shingles still stands in Lviv.

83

WHAT IS ORTHODOX?

Just as the architecture of the church is bound to follow a certain pattern, so too are the church services. The order in which a church service progresses is the same as it has been for centuries. The sermon must always come from the holy books of the Bible. The musical liturgy of the choir has been fixed for every occasion and cannot be chosen randomly. This music is very specific and can only be heard in Orthodox churches. No musical instruments are allowed, and laughter, or even smiling, is prohibited—praying to God is a very serious matter. There are a number of small rules of correct behavior that are absent in many other churches. For example, the accepted way for Orthodox Christians to cross themselves, to light a candle (only from other candles, never with a lighter or matches), to place one's hands (never behind one's back, and never in the pockets), and many others. Ukrainian Orthodox women always cover their heads with kerchiefs when they attend church.

UKRAINIAN BAROQUE CHURCHES

Ukrainian baroque churches were built using a unique style of church architecture, sometimes called Kozak architecture, because it was used between the mid-17th and 18th centuries, the time of the most active Kozak movement. Architecturally, Ukrainian Kozak churches are a blend of Byzantine and western European influences. Kozak churches were made all of wood, the parts joined meticulously without a single nail. Only a few have survived the misfortunes of time: floods, fires, and vandalism. They can be seen in central Ukraine, not far from Kiev, Chernihiv, and Cherkasy.

OTHER RELIGIOUS DENOMINATIONS

It is difficult to know exactly how many of Ukraine's population profess allegiance to the Ukrainian Orthodox Church, (also called the Ukrainian Autocephalous Church) and how many to the Russian Orthodox Church, but together they make up about 65 percent of the country's total population.

The Ukrainian Greek-Catholic Church (sometimes called the Uniate Church) has the second largest following in Ukraine. This denomination originated in 1596 for the benefit of Roman Catholic Poland, which dominated significant parts of Ukraine at the time. The Ukrainian Greek-Catholic Church follows the Eastern rite, while recognizing the leadership of the pope in Rome. There are about 5 million faithful Greek-Catholics, most of whom live in the western part of Ukraine, which was ruled by the Poles for centuries.

Even with mass emigration in recent years, there are still more than 500,000 Jews in Ukraine. Several synagogues serve the Ukrainian Jews.

The Crimea has seen a resurgence of its first peoples, the Tatars. Many have returned home from various places in the former Soviet Union, where they once had been cruelly deported by the Stalin regime. Mosques and Islamic schools are once again becoming popular places for Muslims to gather and practice their religion.

Above: **Muslim boys reading together. The current Ukrainian government is tolerant to all kinds of religious activities provided they bring no harm to society.**

Opposite: **A Ukrainian Orthodox bishop addressing his congregation.**

KIEVO-PECHERSKA LAVRA (THE CAVE MONASTERY)

Kievo-Pecherska Lavra (KIH-ih-voh peh-CHER-skah LAH-vrah) is the oldest monastery in Ukraine, built at the dawn of the Christian era in Kievan Rus. Lavra is a term reserved for monasteries of the highest importance, which are under the direct jurisdiction of the patriarch. Besides Kievo-Pecherska, only one other monastery in western Ukraine has gained the status of lavra. Just as Mecca is a sacred place for Muslims to visit at least once in their lifetime, Kievo-Pecherska Lavra in Kiev has become a sacred place for all Orthodox Christians. The monastery consists of numerous churches, a huge bell tower, dormitories, a maze of caves, underground rooms, and connecting corridors. The original caves were excavated in the 11th century and served not only as places to hide from invaders but also as places to meditate in solitude, isolated from the cruelty and noise of the outside world.

RELIGION TODAY

There were about 80,000 Orthodox churches in the Russian Empire before the Revolution of 1917, of which fewer than 8,000 had survived by 1980.

"They all have hidden crosses on their foreheads," an American concluded about Ukrainians after a long visit to Ukraine some time ago. This observation is fairly astute considering the lengths the Communist regime went to discourage religion. At universities, besides an enormous number of ideological subjects, there was also a mandatory course on "scientific atheism." The subject was organized to prove that there is no God. Anyone who wanted to reach success in their career was forced to pronounce themselves as being an atheist. Religion was seen as the most serious obstacle to spreading Communism.

Things have changed since then, and the cross on the forehead no longer needs to be hidden. Religion has returned to homes and neighborhoods in the form of icons and restored churches. In 1988, even before Ukraine's official independence, Kiev attracted thousands of visitors for the celebration of the Millennium of Christianity in Rus at Kievo-Pecherska Lavra, despite the fact that at the time it was still labeled as a museum.

Although Ukraine still has a long way to go to reestablish prerevolutionary conditions, the liberation of religion there has attracted numerous preachers, missionaries, and prophets from all around the world.

For the younger generation, the return to religion has become a popular trend. What once was considered old-fashioned behavior and denounced by the Communist youth, is today not only condoned, it has been embraced by droves of young Ukrainians.

WITCHCRAFT: BLACK AND WHITE MAGIC

There are many superstitions in Ukraine that are a fusion of pagan and Christian beliefs. Speaking with somebody while standing on the threshold, a black cat's crossing one's path, whistling inside the house—these and many others are said to invite bad luck. Many Ukrainians believe in black magic and its opposing force, white magic. Witches are reputed to have the power to prevent crops from growing or to kill livestock. The witch's curse is also believed to be able to drive its victim to the grave by inexplicable disease or a strange accident. In Ukrainian folktales, though, a brave Kozak always overcomes the curses, devil's temptations, and all kinds of witchcraft by his strong faith, keen wits, and optimism.

LANGUAGE

UKRAINIAN LANGUAGE HAS SUFFERED GREATLY from the influence of the Russian language. Though mutual influence is natural and unavoidable in bordering states, Russian was the official language for the entire Union of Soviet Socialist Republics. That meant that all business correspondence, official communications, and printed newspapers were in Russian. Ukrainians attempted to obtain bilingual passports, licenses, and certificates, but they had little success. National radio stations and television channels were broadcast solely in Russian, and although the Ukrainian mass media were permitted to operate, they were much less influential and pervasive than their Russian counterparts.

Above: **The Kozaks, painted on the wall behind this boy, were the protectors of the Ukrainian language. In the Kozak settlements, men, women, and children were taught to read and write.**

Opposite: **A Ukrainian environmental demonstrator holds aloft a banner against the use of nuclear power at a conference in Kiev, April 24, 2006, devoted to the 20th anniversary of the Chernobyl disaster.**

Attempts to Russify the nation were not limited to language use, but the suppression of language as a crucial emblem of national morale was an important loss. After the fall of the Soviet Union, the revival of the Ukrainian language was one of the first reforms enacted by the Ukrainian parliament.

The problem of language is not that simple a matter to resolve, however. Not only is Ukraine populated by 10 million Russians but many Ukrainians speak better Russian than their own Ukrainian, having been taught Russian in school. In fact, Russian and Ukrainian are very closely related, with a 60 percent shared vocabulary, but for some it is a matter of national pride more than an issue of literacy that Ukrainian be restored as the national language.

A road sign written in Ukrainian. Only since independence has Ukrainian come back into official status.

UKRAINIAN

Ukrainian belongs to the large family of Indo-European languages, along with English, Spanish, and many other modern languages. At the same time, Ukrainian also belongs to the Slavic group, along with Polish, Bulgarian, and Russian, while English is also part of the Germanic group, along with German and Dutch. Therefore, although the Ukrainian and English languages are related, their kinship is rather a distant one.

The relationship, however, is evident in certain words. For example, "two" and "three" in English are *dva* (di-VA) and *try* (tree) in Ukrainian, the English word "beat" is *byty* (BIT-tea) in Ukrainian, and "water" translates as *voda* (VO-da). There are many other words that only comparative linguistics can identify as being related. In some cases it is not clear whether a word has the same origin or was just borrowed from another language (compare the English word "hut" with the Ukrainian *khata* [CA-ta], meaning in both languages approximately the same thing). There are very few words in the English language borrowed from the Ukrainian, but there are many words in Ukrainian that are from English.

Words representing specific activities or items originating in foreign cultures in the last century, such as jazz, jeans, computer, and rock and roll, have been adopted without any changes. There are also words that sound almost identical but mean quite different things, to the confusion of inexperienced translators. For example, the Ukrainian *mahazyn* (ma-ha-ZEEN) means "store," not "magazine."

WRITTEN UKRAINIAN

At the end of the 11th century, the Slavic languages began to exhibit distinct differences from each other. This is usually explained by migration and cultural influences from neighboring countries. Today, it is easy to tell that Russian was influenced by the Scandinavian languages and that Turkic, while still Ukrainian, preserving its Old Slavonic roots, adopted many words from Poland, Russia, and Austria.

The written Ukrainian language originated in the ninth century, when the Byzantine missionary brothers Saint Cyril and Saint Methodius created an alphabet based on Greek and Hebrew letters. This system of characters developed into what is called the Cyrillic alphabet, after Saint Cyril. The Cyrillic alphabet, used by scholarly missionaries to translate the Bible into the Slavic language, is still used today, with some adaptations, by Ukrainians, Russians, Belarussians, Bulgarians, and other Slavic nations.

The Ukrainian alphabet has 33 letters. One letter, the soft sign, does not have its own sound, but makes the preceding consonant "soft," thus changing its pronunciation. There are two features of Ukrainian that make

The Lviv State University library. Admission to advanced education in Ukraine is valued highly.

91

easy for an English speaker to learn: the letters are pronounced exactly the way they are pronounced in the alphabet, regardless of their accented or unaccented position in the word, and the structure of the sentence (syntax) is more flexible than in English, allowing wide stylistic leeway.

MASS MEDIA IN UKRAINE

In a famous Ukrainian joke, a member of an inspection committee asks a randomly picked person in the streets of Kiev, "Do you have everything that you need?" "Yes." "Can you buy everything in state stores?" "Sure." "Do you read newspapers?" "Of course—how else would I know that I have everything?"

The joke illustrates the ridiculous difference between what was written in newspapers and the actual situation in Ukraine before independence. All mass media were state-owned and state-supported. Reporters' material was thoroughly censored by editors who were appointed to their positions and strictly supervised by the Communist Party committee. No matter

There are three Ukrainian greetings, each used depending on the time of day. Dobryy ranok *(DOH-brii RAH-nok), Good morning;* Dobryy den *(DOH-brii DEN'), Good afternoon;* Dobryy vechir *(DOH-brii VEH-chir), Good evening.*

what happened in the country, news was always rosy. The most one could find out about a plane crash, if anything at all, was something like "there were victims." A disaster the size of the Chernobyl nuclear power plant explosion was not mentioned in the press at all. To keep control over such powerful mass media as television and radio, the central leadership prohibited the development of local television stations. Thus there were only two television channels from Moscow and one or two from Kiev available in Ukraine. Crammed with propaganda, the national channels' advantage was the complete absence of commercial advertising. The same was true for radio.

The evolution of private electronic mass media has been slowed by provisions in the Law on Television and Radio Broadcasting that was enacted by parliament in 1994. Constant personnel changes in the State Committee on Television and Radio Broadcasting have caused

A book bazaar in Mariupol, the Donetsk region. Ukrainians take great pride in their home libraries, and governmental education laws mean that nearly 100 percent of Ukrainians are literate.

Reading the newspaper in a park in Kiev. Ukrainians are avid readers and love their free press and their libraries.

bureaucratic delays as well. According to new laws, priority will be given to stations promoting Ukrainian culture and language. The law requires all private television and radio stations to broadcast a minimum of 50 percent domestic content, as opposed to devoting full airtime to powerful satellite services, such as Voice of America or the BBC.

Freedom of the press and electronic mass media is guaranteed by the Ukrainian constitution, a surety that has produced unexpected results. As more and more of newly created print newspapers appeared on the streets (private radio and television developed more slowly), standards and quality fell below what was previously judged as acceptable.

Press freedom has improved since the 2004 Orange Revolution, and there is decreased government intervention in the work of journalists. Their work, however, is still being hampered by the real and persistent threat of injury and even murder. In 2001 Oleh Breus, the publisher of *XXI Vek*—a regional weekly—was shot dead by two gunmen outside his home in Luhansk. In the same year, Ihor Oleksandrov, director of the private television and radio station TOR in Slavyansk, died after four unidentified men attacked him at his office. Oleksandrov's death was believed to be linked to his investigations into corruption and organized crime. In 2004 the director of Radio Yuta in Poltava, Yuriy Chechyk, died in a dubious car crash while on his way to a meeting with executives of Radio Liberty's Ukrainian Service.

Television and radio have introduced massive commercial advertising into every available minute. Many commercials are imported from the West and translated into Ukrainian.

DIALECTS AND NONVERBAL COMMUNICATION

Some of the peculiarities in pronunciation and vocabulary make it easy to distinguish a person from the Poltava area in central Ukraine from his counterpart in the western part of Ukraine, and a person who grew up in the south from one who lives in the east. Subjected to continuous invasions and numerous outside influences, Ukrainians in these areas have developed very distinctive dialects. Of course, not everyone in these regions uses the same language patterns, and a standard Ukrainian speech is used by the media and taught in schools, so there are rarely any problems of miscommunication.

Gestures and instinctive reactions also figure prominently in communication. Ukrainians use their hands, movements of the head, and facial expressions to emphasize the meaning of their words. Some gestures are common outside Ukraine as well, for example, the slight nodding of one's head while listening to a conversation (meaning "I comprehend and agree"); shaking one's head from left to right (meaning "I disagree"); or clapping one's hands (signifying approval and encouragement). Others are unique to Ukraine, such as whistling during concerts and performances to convey disapproval.

A teacher reading to children in a day-care center. Children in Ukraine may be admitted to child-care centers when they are less than one year old, so they learn to communicate with people outside the family when they are very young.

FORMS OF ADDRESS

Since 1921 when the Ukrainian Soviet Socialist Republic was established, the terms Mr. and Mrs. in Ukraine were supplanted by the genderless "comrade." The explanation was that Mr. and Mrs. were used to address people in a superior position, while under Communism everyone is meant to be equal. Today the traditional *pan* (pahn) for Mr., *pani* (PAH-nih) for Mrs., and *panna* (PAH-nah) for Miss are gradually replacing comrade. Which form of address is the appropriate one, however, is temporarily a puzzle for Ukrainians, who, to avoid any bias, quite often use no salutation at all in letters besides the name.

There are two ways to say "you" in Ukrainian: the formal *vy* and the familiar *ty*. The second, as a rule, is used between people who address each other by their first names, which does not happen as readily in Ukraine as it does in North America. It is rude to call someone by only their first or last name if it is the first meeting. The first name in combination with the patronymic name is the best approach. For example, Ivan Mykolayovych

PROVERBS IN COMPARISON

Every country in the world uses proverbs to illustrate life's lessons. A comparison of proverbs in Ukrainian and English demonstrates the similarities that abound across borders.

Ukrainian: *Ridna zemlya i v zhmeni myla.* (Native soil is dear even if it is only a handful.)
English: Be it ever so humble, there is no place like home.

Ukrainian: *Nasha syla—sim'ya yedyna.* (Our strength is in the united family.)
English: United we stand, divided we fall.

Ukrainian: *Khto rano posiye, toy rano y pozhne.* (Those who plant early will harvest early.)
English: The early bird catches the worm.

Ukrainian: *Iz vohniu ta v polum'ya.* (Out of the flames into the fire.)
English: Out of the frying pan and into the fire.

is the appropriate way to address a man whose father's last name was Mykolayovy, or Tetyana Petrivna for a woman whose father's name was Petriv.

TATAR

The Tatar language is part of the northwestern or Kipchak Turkic language group, including Kirgiz, Nogay, Kazakh, Kara-Kalpak, Kumyk, Bashkir, Karaim, Karachay, and Balkar. The development of a distinct Turkic language began in the eighth century in Inner Asia (primarily Central Asia, Mongolia, and Tibet). Arabic script was generally used by all Turkic peoples until the early 1920s, when Latin script was adopted by the Turkic peoples of the USSR. After 1939, Latin script was almost completely replaced in the USSR by modern forms of the Cyrillic alphabet. The Arabic alphabet is still used by Turkic peoples living in China and the Arab countries.

One of the most distinctive features of Turkic languages is vowel harmony. There are two kinds of vowels, front vowels, produced at the front of the mouth (e, i, ö, ü), and back vowels, produced at the back of the mouth (a, o, u). Vowel harmony has been broken down in some languages, but purely Turkic words contain either all front or all back vowels. Word formation is governed by agglutination, which is the use of suffixes, rather than independent words, to express grammatical concepts. For example, the word *evlerimde* (in my house), is composed of *ev* (house), *ler* (plural suffix), *im* (possessive suffix of first person singular), *de* (location suffix in).

A monument in Lviv to the first book printer in Russia, Ivan Fiodorov.

ARTS

TWO MAIN FORCES drove the development of art in Ukraine: service to God and the desire to express emotion through decoration and depiction of the environment. Popular motifs were derived from the various stages in Ukraine's history. From the mysterious Trypillyan culture came the spiral, repeated again and again as a symbol of the ongoing creation of life; swastikas painted on hard-cooked eggs were an expression of the ancient Sanskrit symbol of never-ending progress; circles represented the sun, the most important of the pagan gods; crosses were embroidered in cloth to guard and protect the name of the Savior. Foreign conquerors attempted to suppress these art forms, but the oppression only strengthened the folk art movement as an expression of national identity.

RELIGIOUS ICONS

Service to God in art is characterized best of all by a variety of church icons, small religious paintings. To make an icon, a wooden panel was sanded down until the surface was clean and smooth. The paints were made from a base of egg yolks and other natural ingredients, but the original recipe was lost long ago. The oldest surviving icons in Ukraine, painted in the 11th century, depict events in the Bible and saints in Eastern Orthodox history. These early paintings can be seen at Kiev's Saint Sofia Cathedral.

The craft of the *bohomaz* (boh-hoh-MAHZ), as the artists were called, was well respected, but contrary to popular belief, the artists were not. In fact, very often they were serfs working for a landlord who would permit them to contract work with churches and give them only a small share of the payment collected.

Above: **A painted icon depicting the Annunciation displayed in a church in Lviv.**

Opposite: **Street musicians playing the violin and flute outside the Odessa theater.**

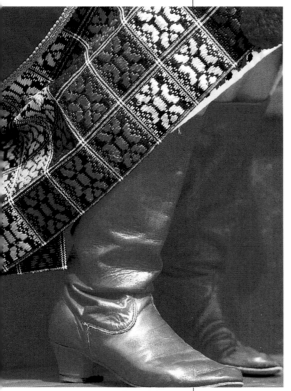

Intricately embroidered patterns are a trademark of Ukrainian fiber art.

EMBROIDERY

For hundreds of years, Ukrainian women have devoted long winter nights to weaving, embroidering, and attaching complicated bead designs to their clothing. Traditionally, mothers and their daughters embroidered a shirt, handkerchief, or tobacco pouch for their husbands, sons, or sweethearts. Floral designs were embroidered on towels and napkins that were hung in the kitchen and throughout the house. Embroidery can also be found in the interior of churches on altar cloths and hangings, and in priests' vestments.

Embroidery is a long process demanding time and patience. Different parts of the country have their own unique patterns, but black and red threads against a white background are the prevailing colors throughout the land.

"Red for love, black for sorrow." Red and black are traditional colors in many fields of Ukrainian art, representing life's two polarities.

POTTERY

While initially pottery making was a practical way of equipping a kitchen with necessary tableware and containers, later it grew into an art form. Recently, traditional pottery is regaining popularity in Ukraine. Folk art items are beginning to appear in Ukrainian homes to replace standard commercial goods. There are large deposits of many varieties of clays throughout Ukraine, which has been a major factor in the growth and development of this art.

EASTER EGGS

The art of decorating eggs in the spring has become associated with Easter over the years, but this art form existed long before Christianity came to Ukraine. In many countries around the world, spring is a celebration of new life, and Ukrainians believe there is a great power in the new life embodied in an egg. Ancient legends of many cultures tell of a giant egg from which the universe emerged. Eggs were believed to have the power to heal, protect, and to bring good luck and wealth. Such beliefs are the reason behind the tradition of keeping a plateful of decorated eggs in the home.

After the introduction of Christianity to Ukraine, the art of egg decorating continued to develop. Today there are two types of decorated Easter eggs. The simpler one, called *krashanka* (KRAH-shahn-kah), is an edible hard-cooked egg painted with one bright color (*kraska*, pronounced KRAHS-kah, is the root word, from the Slavic for "paint"). The more detailed *pysanka* (PIH-sahn-kah), is made from a raw egg whose contents have been removed, painted with various colors and designs, and kept in the house as decoration. The difference can be seen most clearly in the root word *pysaty* (pih-SAH-tih), meaning "to write."

The long, careful procedure used in making *pysanka* eggs is one of the things that makes them so beautiful. The design, determined ahead of time, is drawn in wax on the surface of the egg. Then the egg is dipped in different colored dyes, from brightest to darkest, with new wax

It is a Ukrainian tradition to keep Easter eggs in the house throughout the year to ward off evil and to invite health and wealth.

being applied between dippings. The wax pattern seals the color, so the artist must keep the image of the final design in mind at all times—it is impossible to "rewrite" anything on the surface of the egg. Before the final step, when the wax is heated and wiped from the egg, the design cannot be seen. In fact, the egg looks most unattractive. This makes the impression even stronger when the miracle of the artist's creation suddenly appears the moment the wax is removed.

Traditionally, the dyes were made of various herbs and plants, including sunflower seeds, walnuts, buckwheat husks, moss, and birch leaves. Today, the dyes can be bought as powder and mixed as desired. The *kistka* (KIST-kah), or stylus, the tool used for drawing the wax pattern has also been updated. In the old days, the stylus was filled with wax and then had to be warmed by the flame of a candle every minute to ensure that the wax did not cool. Now there are electric styluses of various sizes that, when plugged in, keep the wax always hot.

MUSIC

Ukrainian is a very melodious language. But the "singsong" sound of the language only partially explains why Ukrainians like to sing so much. Music is inevitably a part of any party or get-together, used to express both joy and sorrow.

Ukrainian music developed from a basis of folk songs, many of them composed and spread by *kobzars* (kob-ZAHRS), bards who traveled from town to town performing their music. The name *kobzar* was derived from the name of the musical instrument they used to accompany their songs. The *kobza* is an ancient Ukrainian instrument (very much like a round lute with three or four strings), a predecessor of the *bandura* (bahn-DOO-rah), another stringed musical instrument. The

bandura, which is asymmetrical in shape and contains up to 60 strings, became popular in the 17th century. In the Carpathian Mountains one can also play the *trembita* (trem-BEE-tah), a wind instrument with a profoundly mournful sound. Made in the shape of a cylindrical tube, *trembitas* can be as long as 10 feet (3 m).

Unlike in other countries, Ukrainian folk music has never, till recently, merged with popular music. There have been several attempts in recent years to create a uniquely Ukrainian rock-and-roll genre, and one success story is found in Ruslana. Known by only her first name, Ruslana won the Eurovision song contest in 2004 with her inspiring mix of traditional Ukrainian music and modern rock.

Some of the most famous Ukrainian folk singers are Nina Matviyenko, Raisa Kyrychenko, and Anatoliy Solov'yanenko. Mykola Lysenko, a passionate promoter of Ukrainian music, and Mykola Leontovych, the composer of the world-famous *Carol of the Bells*, are other well-known Ukrainian musicians.

A performance in the famous Opera House in Odessa.

DANCE

Dance, as a form of art or simply as entertainment, is very popular in Ukraine. Folk dances vary in style, depending on the region. In the west, group dances made up of both men and women are popular. The ritual meanings of the dances have been lost in time, and today they are usually danced to commemorate important events (weddings, in particular) and to entertain the public.

What is known to the world as Kozak dancing indeed originated with the Kozaks of the 16th century but not as a dance at all. The vigorous movements were part of a regime of calisthenics to keep the Kozaks fit for battle. Not until much later was the discipline transformed into a group dance with leaps, rapid movements, and comic improvisations. This dance is called the *hopak* (hoh-PAHK), and it can be performed only by very well-trained artists. One of the best professional groups in Ukraine is the Hopak Kiev Dance Troop.

LITERATURE, FILM, AND THEATER

Ukrainian writers and poets (with the possible exception of Taras Shevchenko) are not generally known internationally. This is due largely to the suppression of Ukrainian culture in the 18th and 19th centuries. Literature was the most powerful instrument in an ongoing struggle to promote Ukrainian nationalism. Ukrainians remember with gratitude such names as Ivan Franko, Yuriy Kotsubynskyy, Marko Vovchok, and many others. When it was forbidden to write in Ukrainian, these were the few who continued to do so despite the consequences. Other Ukrainian writers were forced to write in Russian, but most never forgot their roots.

Ukrainian drama never reached a golden age, but opera was popular. Mykola Lysenko, talented composer and author of the historical opera *Taras Bulba*, and Semen Hulak-Artemovskyy, composer of *The Kozak Beyond the Danube*, are two well-known Ukrainians whose operas are still performed in theaters throughout Ukraine.

Ukraine has three major film studios, in Kiev, Odessa, and Kharkiv. One of the most prominent moviemakers, Oleksandr Dovzhenko (the Kiev film studio was named after him), was accused by the Soviets of the promotion of Ukrainian nationalism. The Ukrainian film industry has many gifted and popular actors who are recognized within the former USSR and internationally.

During the years of Soviet domination, prose was not forbidden, but no literature directed at the development of Ukrainian culture was tolerated. Since independence, the government has given priority to the cultivation of Ukrainian literature.

Hopak dancing is a widely admired folk art, performed here by skilled dancers.

LEISURE

THE SWITCH FROM DAILY LABOR to anticipated leisure in Ukraine is not as smooth as it is in other countries. Ukrainians prefer to work as hard as possible to complete a task in one attempt, no matter how long it takes, in order to have their leisure totally dissociated from nagging thoughts of unfinished work.

Ukrainians spend their free time carefully, making the most of time off. Picnics are a popular way of combining the relaxation of eating, drinking, singing, and getting fresh air. Movies, plays, and ballet are great weekend activities if tickets are available. Prices for excellent classical concerts, operas, and stage productions are relatively inexpensive, often priced at just a few dollars even at the National Opera in Kiev.

Unfortunately, as in many places, weekends are most often the only time for people to take care of chores at home. That is why for many people painting, gardening, laundry, cleaning, and general household maintenance and repairs have become leisure activities.

Left: **The rolling hills of central and western Ukraine enable challenging hiking in the midst of beautiful scenery.**

Opposite: **Open-air strolling and stopping for snacks is a favorite pastime in Kiev.**

A festive family dinner. All generations of Ukrainians love good food and the socializing that goes with it.

AT HOME

There are folks in Ukraine who could easily qualify as "couch potatoes," with only one difference—it is not so much that they are chained to the couch but that they have a love of the home in general. "Let's get together on Saturday, our place," is a typical weekend invitation that is extended spontaneously to a friend during a telephone conversation on Friday. The invitation is usually accepted or rejected on the spot. For Ukrainians, eating is a form of leisure. Having a meal is not just a way to satisfy one's hunger, it is also a time to chat with friends and family about the day's events or the political situation. Relatives may often get together for dinner once or twice a week, with the whole family pitching in to help with the food arrangements.

TELEVISION AND NEWSPAPERS

Spending evenings in front of the television has become routine leisure for many Ukrainian families. Recently, a few international channels and substantially more specialized cable channels have become available. Parents are becoming concerned about their children's leisure time, because watching television competes with friends, homework, reading, and outdoor play for their attention.

Today, newspapers provide as much choice in entertainment as television does. There are dozens of different papers dedicated to a wide variety of topics, from politics to sports.

SPORTS

Sports complexes are found in every large city in Ukraine. These complexes usually house a swimming pool and facilities for aerobics, boxing, and team games. For students, there are sports academies or their own secondary school facilities. If nothing else is available, simply a flat grassy surface somewhere in a park will work well for soccer games.

Sailing is a popular pastime for many Ukrainians, particularly in summer.

Adults are also taking part in amateur sports competitions. The most popular amateur sports are soccer, basketball, volleyball, hockey, and boxing. Tennis is slowly making its way to Ukraine and, more recently, martial arts such as karate and kung fu. Golfers will be disappointed that there is only one major golf course in the whole country, although there are lesser ones associated with hotels.

Ukrainian athletes were some of the strongest members of the Soviet Olympic teams. Some of these athletes have gained worldwide recognition, such as pole-vaulter Serhiy Bubka, gymnasts Tetiana Hutsul and Hryhory Misyutin, and figure skaters Oksana Baiul and Viktor Petrenko, to name only a few. Ukrainians also are proud of their world-class professional boxers, such as Taras Bidenko, Sergey Danilchenko, Sergey Dotsenko, Vitali Klitschko, Wladimir Klitschko, Andreas Kotelnik, and Wladimir Sidorenko, all of whom have won many Olympic medals in the sport.

Since its independence, Ukraine has been participating in both the Summer and Winter Olympics. In the 2004 Summer Olympics in Athens, the country's athletes took home 23 medals (9 gold, 5 silver, and 9 bronze).

Soccer is the national sport of Ukraine, and there are many Ukrainian international soccer stars, notably Andriy Shevchenko, who played on the AC Milan team. In 2006, for the first time in its football (as soccer is called) history, Ukraine qualified for the FIFA (International Federation of Association Football) World Cup in Germany and made it to the semifinals of that tournament. Many young Ukrainian boys dream of becoming famous soccer players on the Kiev Dynamo team. On the day of the final game in a championship match, all regular activity comes to a halt while fans nationwide watch the action on TV or listen to the coverage on the radio.

A young boy out with his bike near the village of Spac.

Cycling is also a popular pastime. For many people living in towns, bicycles are a means of transportation, especially appreciated in the days of fuel shortages. More serious cyclists participate in organized bicycle marathons. Though there are few special bicycle paths and trails, the traffic in Ukraine is fairly light, which makes cycling on city streets a safe and convenient way to travel and get some exercise at the same time.

A traditional marathon takes place in Odessa every year, dedicated to the anniversary of the city's liberation in 1944 from Nazi occupation during World War II. The participants follow a route, called the Circle of Glory, or Feodosiya, that passes by each of the monuments to the defenders of the city. People of all ages take part in patriotic shared events like this one.

TRAVEL

Vacation time begins as soon as the weather turns warm, usually from the middle of May until the middle of August. Some Ukrainians plan

their vacations ahead of time by booking a tour package through a travel agency. Other people go to resorts by the sea or take what are called "wild" vacations in Ukraine, meaning they drive to their chosen destination, pitch a tent, and cook their food over a campfire. The absence of laws for private land ownership makes camping like this possible, but local governments in seaside towns do their best to keep the hordes of "wild" tourists to a minimum.

International destinations have long been the dream of many Ukrainian travelers. In the past, because of tight political repression and the lack of ready cash, such trips were destined to remain dreams. Ukrainians today are free to travel the world, but for the majority of the population, international travel is still too costly. One pleasant outcome of independence is that a large number of emigrants have come home to visit their relatives, which they couldn't do before.

Sunbathers at the beach in Simeiz, a Crimean health resort on the Black Sea.

Many popular resorts are nestled along the Ukrainian part of the Black Sea and the shores of the Sea of Azov. The largest is Odessa, where the population of one million more than doubles during the summer months. The Crimean Peninsula has Yalta, Feodosiya, Alushta, and all the seashore in between for spas, hotels, and beautiful beaches. Several places on the Sea of Azov with its shallow warm waters offer good accommodations as well.

REST HOMES AND SANATORIUMS

There are two types of facilities designed specifically for relaxation, leisure, and health restoration—rest homes and sanatoriums, which are somewhat like spas in the West. Although neither is equipped to deal with specialized health problems, medical personnel are available to make guests feel secure and cared for.

Most guests stay for a period of three weeks and are provided with comfortable rooms, good food and entertainment, and therapeutic treatment, such as massages, mud baths, or physical exercise on a daily basis by trained specialists. These establishments are generally located in quiet, picturesque places away from the hubbub of large cities. Formerly subsidized by state funds, the facilities were easily affordable for many Ukrainians. Since the introduction of the self-supporting system, however, many of these health retreats have become rather expensive.

ALONE WITH NATURE

Some people's idea of a perfect vacation is to escape the city crowds and surround themselves with nature. Though Ukraine is a densely populated country, it is still possible to find an isolated spot on the bank of a river or lake to fish, camp, and swim.

Others, desiring something more adventurous, find white-water rafting down Ukraine's major rivers a thrilling sport. During the summer months, elaborate rafts with single adventurers or whole families can be seen on the Dnister, Dnipro, or Privdennyy Bug rivers.

For winter vacation enthusiasts, there are many resort areas, especially in the Carpathian Mountains. For those interested in skiing, there is no better place than Yaremcha in western Ukraine, renowned for its beauty, delicious food, and spas, not to mention the excellent ski slopes.

Having lunch on a hike in the Carpathian Mountains in western Ukraine.

FESTIVALS

THERE ARE TWO TYPES of holidays in Ukraine—religious and political. In the past, political holidays were celebrated on the anniversaries of the Russian Revolution of 1917, on the date when the latest version of the constitution was adopted, and on May 1, as an expression of the solidarity of the working classes of the world. Religious holidays were not officially celebrated at all, but unofficially, people observed them the way their ancestors had done for centuries. The holidays were listed on the church calendar, issued by the Ukrainian Orthodox patriarch's office every year.

All the changes in the political, economic, and cultural life of Ukrainians have been reflected in their holidays. Holidays with political significance to the former USSR are generally not celebrated anymore.

Left: **Marchers in a parade at a Ukrainian folk festival.**

*Opposite***: Dancers wearing traditional costumes at a Ukrainian festival.**

Religious festivals have taken their place. All in all, independence has meant that, happily, there are more red numbers (indicating days off) on the calendar than in the old days.

REMEMBERING THE WAR

Many people are puzzled when they see the size of World War II memorials in Ukraine. One in Kiev, for example, is larger than the famous Cave Monastery. The central monument, a woman holding a sword, symbolizing the country ready to defend itself, is almost as tall as the tallest bell tower in the monastery. Ukrainians may differ on the subject of expenditure on war memorials, but 5 million Ukrainians died in World War II, a catastrophe that touched virtually every family in the country.

Victory Day, May 9, is a tribute to the countless soldiers who gave their lives defending Ukraine. It is also an antiwar holiday, a moving reminder of the atrocities of war. Flowers are carried to memorials, which can be found in every city and village in Ukraine. Veterans wear their decorations and gather together to share their memories. Once, only the veterans of the Soviet army took to the streets on this day, but since independence, veterans of the Ukrainian Liberation Army (who fought both the German and Soviet armies in western Ukraine) freely celebrate Victory Day. Today, younger people in uniforms, veterans of the war in Afghanistan, can be seen mingling with the Liberation Army veterans and the venerable veterans of World War II.

INTERNATIONAL WOMEN'S DAY

March 8 is a holiday for all women, mothers first and foremost. The holiday was established by a German Communist Party leader named Clara Zetkin to commemorate the struggle for women's rights. Over the years much of its political meaning has faded, and today it is comparable to Mother's Day in other countries. Husbands, boyfriends, fathers, and sons do their best to make this day as enjoyable as possible for women. Most families try to do something special for mother by preparing a special dinner, making a card, or giving her flowers. International Women's Day is a national holiday in Ukraine.

May 1 used to be celebrated as the International Day of Workers' Solidarity. In the USSR there were "demonstrations of solidarity" on that date. Today, the political meaning of May Day is somewhat forgotten, and instead, people simply celebrate the arrival of spring. Older Ukrainians, however, may still be heard singing worker songs on this day.

THE AFGHANISTAN WAR

When the Soviet Union rolled into Afghanistan in 1979, an official report was issued stating that the USSR intended to provide help to a group of struggling Afghans at their request. Nobody in the USSR expected the involvement to grow into a full-scale war that would last more than 10 years. Beginning in 1980, service in Afghanistan became a mandatory part of "real war" training for young military professionals, from which many of them returned in zinc coffins.

There was no choice for the 18-year-old boys drafted for compulsory army service. Tens of thousands of them died in Afghanistan, and hundreds of thousands returned with physical and mental scars. The veterans from Afghanistan in Ukraine formed what is called "the lost generation." When the young soldiers finally came home, they found it extremely difficult to readjust to life in a peaceful environment.

Opposite: **The huge Defense of the Motherland Monument in Kiev was built by the Soviets.**

Kolach (**KO-latch**) is special bread baked for festive occasions and Christmas. The candle represents Jesus Christ, light of the world.

CHRISTMAS

Ukrainians celebrate Christmas on January 7, the date of Christ's birth according to the Eastern Orthodox calendar. On Christmas Eve, churches hold special services based on ancient rituals. The priests robe in colorful garments of silver and gold, and the choirs perform treasured old hymns. After the service, family members gather at the home of one of them for a festive dinner. The tradition of Christmas caroling is a long one. The prerevolutionary tradition was to present the carolers with food (sausages and bread) and a shot of *horilka* (hoh-RIL-kah), Ukrainian vodka. Today, caroling is still alive and well in Ukraine, and long before Christmas Eve people make sure there are enough cookies, candies, and small coins for all the carolers. Greetings from the visiting group can be in the form of a short poem or song wishing household members happiness and health. These days it is difficult to believe that it was only a few years ago that all religious holidays were officially prohibited. Older people still remember the circles of activists who surrounded churches on Christmas Eve to prevent children (who had been forced to be members of the Young Communist League) from watching the service.

EASTER

Another important religious holiday is Easter. Preparations for the holiday begin 40 days before Easter Sunday, on Ash Wednesday. The Lenten season is rather strict—the faithful do not eat meat or animal fat for 40 days, and avoid cheese and oils for seven days before Easter Sunday. Everything at home must be cleaned and decorated for Easter, inside and out. There are several solemn pre-Easter church services, with the culmination on Easter Sunday. Each family brings a basket of food to the church on Sunday morning to be blessed with holy water by the priest. After the food has been blessed, everyone goes home to break the fast. On Easter Sunday it is customary to greet people with the words "Christ is risen" to which they answer, "He is risen, indeed!"

The weekend after Easter is a family memorial time. Families make their way to their ancestral burial plots, clean and arrange the area, spend a quiet moment in remembrance of their loved ones, and have a picnic. Burial sites often have benches and tables installed for this custom.

Priests blessing baskets of food on Easter morning. This is a time to forgive sins and set aside anger.

NEW YEAR

During the years when celebrating Christmas was prohibited, New Year became a very important holiday. In fact, today New Year is probably considered the biggest holiday of the year. Ukrainians put up New Year trees, which they decorate with all kinds of ornaments. The trees came to be known as New Year trees because although they are decorated as if to celebrate Christmas, they are taken into the house only a few days before the new year and stand until January 13. This is a special day for some Ukrainians who still celebrate "Old New Year," the start of the new year according to the old calendar, abolished long ago by Peter the Great.

New Year is a time for family reunions, and people travel long distances to be with their relatives at this time of year. New Year is symbolic of the beginning of a new and better life, and even the wildest dreams are believed to come true on this day.

New Year's Eve is full of laughter, goodwill, and entertainment, with much eating, drinking, dancing, and playing of games. Many revelers celebrate throughout the night, and do not go to bed at all.

OTHER HOLIDAYS

Palm Sunday is the first day of Holy Week and the Sunday before Easter. In Ukraine, a Palm Sunday procession moves from a church where the palms are blessed to a church where the liturgies are sung.

A relatively new tradition is to celebrate the Day of the City. For some newer cities, like Odessa, which celebrated only its bicentennial in 1994, it is easy to calculate the day of its founding. For other cities, people must guess. For example, Kiev is estimated to be 1,500 years old. Whether or not the date is correct, everyone enjoys the colorful annual festivals.

THE HOLIDAY OF TRINITY

Although it is not a day off, Trinity is the most important religious holiday after Christmas and Easter. It is celebrated in June, when the trees are green and beautiful, and for this reason it is often called "the green holiday." According to the scriptures, the Holy Spirit appeared before the apostles on the 50th day after Jesus Christ's resurrection and granted them the ability to speak all of the world's languages in order to preach the world over.

Friends and family visit one another on this day and enjoy festive meals. The interiors of homes are decorated with fresh green grass, fragrant herbs, and tree branches, symbolizing the flourishing of life.

FOOD

FOOD HAS ALWAYS HELD SPECIAL MEANING for the people of the breadbasket of Europe. Ukrainians take eating very seriously and, particularly when there is a guest in the house, the preparation of meals requires special efforts. Most meals are labor-intensive, and the dishes are very decorative. Not only is the flavor of the food important, the whole sensation of the meal, from the table setting to the crockery to the complementary colors of the food, is very carefully considered.

Like many other countries in the world, Ukraine has suffered food shortages, and the famine that ravaged the land in the 1930s is still fresh in the minds of many seniors. The rich black soil, however, has bountifully provided Ukraine with the means to feed itself and others, and all Ukrainians are thankful for this.

Above: **Selling broad beans and carrots in a typical Ukrainian outdoor market.**

Opposite: **Women carrying bread for sale at the indoor municipal market in Kiev.**

FRUITS AND VEGETABLES

There has never been an abundance of fruit in Ukraine, but apples, cherries, plums, and other fruits grown in temperate climates are readily available. The same is true of vegetables—many Ukrainians have never heard of avocados, parsnips, sweet potatoes, sweet peas, or green beans, to say nothing of exotic leeks. Due to the political trade regulations of the "iron curtain," imported fruits and vegetables were limited to Cuban oranges. In those days, most Ukrainians had only read of bananas, pineapples, and coconuts. Today almost every possible tropical fruit and vegetable is in their markets.

Visitors to Ukraine would be shocked, though, at the high prices of imported produce—at least twice the price on the world market. But when domestic fruits, nuts, and vegetables are in season, they are "dirt cheap."

Because Ukraine's agricultural infrastructure is not developed enough to provide fresh produce year-round, seasonal canning is very common. Jams, concentrated fruit drinks, tomatoes, cucumbers, and many other food items are pickled or canned to be consumed in winter and spring, a vital necessity in most Ukrainian households. Almost every house and apartment complex is equipped with a cellar or cabinet where jams and pickled vegetables are stored.

A fruit market in Kiev. Imported fruits cost twice as much as domestically-produced ones.

NATIONAL CUISINE

The best of East and West are combined in Ukrainian food. In general, the Ukrainian diet is fairly high in cholesterol, and the health-conscious diner would probably look aghast at it. Compared with diets in Central Asia, like Turkmenistan and Kazakhstan, though, Ukrainian food might be considered lean.

Ukrainians like spicy food and tend to add more pepper, salt, hot paprika, and dill than German or British palates prefer. A Mexican or Korean, though, would likely find the food mild. Ukrainians cook a variety of meat cutlets, hot grains (including buckwheat, a grain that has almost been forgotten in the West except for pancakes), meat rolls, and milk products. Ukrainians are most famous for borscht (BORSH), beet soup. But do not let the plain name disappoint you, because red beets are only one of the many ingredients that make up this delicious and nutritious soup.

Some of the other traditional Ukrainian dishes are *holubtsi* (hoh-loob-TSIH), rolls of cabbage, rice, and ground meat; *varenyki* (vah-REH-nih-kih), dumplings with fruit, potato, or mushroom filling; *deruny* (deh-roo-NIH), blintzes made of ground potatoes and flour; *pyrohy* (pih-roh-HIH), dumplings with various fillings; and a variety of meat (mainly pork) products, especially cured meats. Ukrainians love *rybatska yushka* (rih-BAHTS-kah YUSH-kah), a fish soup that a skillful fisherman can make over an open fire. *Solyanka*, a kind of pickle soup, and *pilmeny*, or meat dumplings, are also prominent in Ukrainian cuisine.

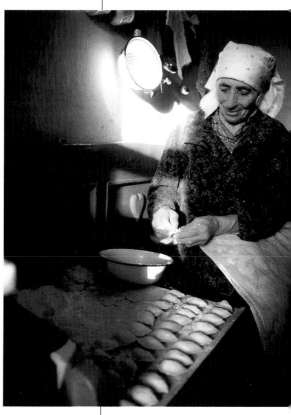

Making *pyrohy (pero-gies)*, dumplings filled with meat, vegetables, or sweets.

While oysters, snails, or frogs' legs are foods many people in Ukraine would consider disgusting (though many have never had a chance to try them), they do not hesitate to prepare beef or pork liver, tongue, lungs, kidneys, brains, and even stewed bulls' tails, which are a rare delicacy. Hogs' trotters (pigs' feet) are widely used by cooks and homemakers to make jellied minced meat or aspic. Liver pie (ground liver mixed with fried onions and other ingredients, fried in the shape of pancakes, and arranged in layers) is also considered a tasty delicacy in the Ukrainian cuisine.

DRINKS

Coffee drinking is seasonal in Ukraine, partly because coffee is not a traditional regional drink, and also because it is not as affordable. Although coffee drinking has yet to fully infiltrate the Ukrainian market

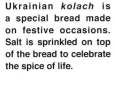

Ukrainian *kolach* is a special bread made on festive occasions. Salt is sprinkled on top of the bread to celebrate the spice of life.

and lifestyle, it has been made more available to shoppers today and is served in virtually every café. Its increasing popularity has also led to an increased demand for instant coffee, especially among the more affluent. Tea is greatly preferred, but iced tea is a strange concept to Ukrainians, who cannot imagine drinking tea any other way than hot. Juices, particularly apple, cherry, birch, and apricot, are popular in the summer, as well as carbonated soft drinks and Russian *kvas* (a fermented bread drink). Milk is drunk everywhere year-round.

Each morning the "milk man" comes around to each farmhouse collecting fresh milk.

ENTERTAINING AT HOME

On special occasions, the dining table is usually covered with an embroidered white tablecloth, crystal glassware, and traditional decorations. People are seated in random order, although some reserve the ends of a rectangular table for special guests. Traditionally, guests were seated so that no two men or two women were next to each other. Today, seating is more casual.

ALCOHOL

Ninety-nine percent of festive dinners are served with alcohol. From time to time, guests will propose a toast, usually to the health of the hosts, to friendship, and to prosperity. The procedure of drinking *horilka*, as vodka is called, at such feasts is different from that in many other cultures. Nobody drinks just when they please, and nobody just sips their drink. The glasses are kept filled at all times.

UKRAINIAN HORILKA

A festive table in Ukraine is impossible to imagine without some kind of alcohol, particularly *horilka*, wine, or, at the very least, beer. Horilka is rarely mixed in a cocktail, instead it is consumed as it is, without ice, in a shot of approximately 2 to 4 ounces. The only stipulation is that the bottle must be very well cooled in advance.

Not surprisingly, alcoholism has become a big social problem in Ukraine. Attempts to curb the consumption of alcohol have been largely unsuccessful. The most recent attempt to limit production and sale of vodka in favor of dry wines, in 1985, known as Gorbachev's Prohibition, resulted in a massive demolition of grape vineyards. As a result, grape juice and wine production dropped significantly, but there was little or no impact on vodka production.

By law, people under the age of 21 are not permitted to buy alcohol, but in reality, few merchants pay attention to the age of the customer and are almost never punished if caught.

Ukraine is not yet integrated into the system of world food distribution. Foreigners are unlikely to find many food or drink items common in the rest of the world. Even Coke and Pepsi are scarce.

A toast must be proposed before the glasses are emptied. When the toast is over, people usually clink their glasses (at least the first time) and drink—bottoms up! If and when someone starts "cheating" (that is, leaving some vodka in the glass), he or she is urged to finish the glass. It is close to impossible to refuse. Unlike in Georgia and Armenia, however, it is not an insult to the host to refuse. Women are allowed to turn their vodka glasses down. It is not unusual for each person to drink a half-liter bottle (about a quart) of vodka during a dinner party.

Alcohol is also a very important part of Ukrainian hospitality. Social norms dictate that the hosts offer unlimited amounts of alcohol on special occasions. Visitors to Ukraine are advised to not compete with Ukrainians in a drinking contest. One of the secrets of staying sober is to eat as much food as possible between toasts.

Beer and wine are also manufactured in Ukraine. Vineyards in the Crimea produce delicious dry wines, but these are generally not as popular as the traditional *horilka* and are rarely taken with meals, particularly celebratory meals. Beer is sold throughout Ukraine. Sometimes it is available on the streets, drawn from large portable tanks.

EATING OUT

Eating out in Ukraine is not nearly as popular as it is in other European countries. Restaurant dining is very expensive, and the quality of food, by and large, is not very good. More importantly, restaurants are not generally restricted to eating. Over the years, they have become places to go for a drink, rather than for a meal. Most Ukrainian waiters would be puzzled by an order for food and soft drinks, since it is a far better value to eat at home.

An accurate picture of most Ukrainian restaurants is loud music, merry singing, and lots of cigarette smoke. Recently, though, more and more private restaurants are catering to a quieter sort of clientele.

Since Ukraine was a closed society for so many years, there are very few ethnic restaurants where diners can try different varieties of regional foods. Ethnic food is still prepared primarily in the home, where, depending on the hosts' backgrounds, one may be served Georgian *shashlyk* (shahsh-LIK), better known as shish kebab in the West; Russian *pelmeni* (pel-meh-nih), meat dumplings; or Uzbekian (Turkic) rice pilaf.

Enjoying an evening out at a café in Kiev.

BORSCHT

Borscht, the national dish of Ukraine, is usually the first course served in a Ukrainian meal. This beet soup has been adopted by other countries in the region, but as recently as 45 years ago, it could not even be found in restaurants in other Soviet republics. There are as many as 30 versions of borscht served throughout the country, which reflects the individuality of Ukrainians as well as their ingenuity. It can contain as many as 20 different ingredients, depending on the season, region, and personal preferences of the cook. It can be meatless or prepared with a rich meat stock featuring either beef or smoked pork.

Beets are the principal ingredient in borscht, giving the soup its distinctive color and pleasing aroma. Borscht originated as a one-pot meal and can be served hot or cold. At its most complex it is a lavish Ukrainian specialty and at its most contemporary an elegantly chilled consommé (a clear soup made from clarified meat stock that often includes vegetables). Ukrainian borscht is borscht at its most extravagant. It can take several days to prepare, is made in large amounts, and is a dish fit for a feast!

UKRAINIAN BORSCHT (BEET SOUP)

Vegetable oil, as needed
1½ to 2 pounds (0.68 to 0.91 kg) stewing beef, cut into small pieces
8 to 10 cups water
beets, a bunch (usually 5 to 6), pared and cut into thin slices, quartered
2 medium onions, chopped
3 large carrots, pared and chopped
16 ounces (453.6 g) sour cream
Salt as desired
Black pepper, coarsely ground, as desired
Dash of vinegar

In a large pan, place enough oil to coat. Add the beef. Begin to brown the meat, stirring frequently and adding water a little at a time so the meat does not burn or stick. After the meat is well browned, add the rest of the water and about 2 teaspoons of salt and bring to a boil. Turn down the heat to medium, cover the pot, and let it simmer for another 30 minutes. Then stir in all the vegetables and cover the pot again. Let the mixture simmer for at least an hour.

During this period, add the amount of black pepper and any more salt you desire. Leave the pot covered and simmer for yet another hour for the flavors of the ingredients to fuse. Before serving, slowly add the sour cream to the soup, stirring and blending it in so there are no lumps. Let the cream melt into the broth. Next, add a dash of vinegar and stir it into the soup. Taste and see if more salt or vinegar is needed. Serve with warm fresh bread. Serves four.

UKRANIAN GRAIN PUDDING (*KUTIA*)

Kutia, a lightly sweetened baked pudding, is the first of 12 traditional dishes served on Christmas Eve in Ukraine. It can be made with wheat berries or barley.

1½ cups pearl barley
¾ cup poppy seeds
½ cup sliced almonds
½ cup honey
½ teaspoon salt
7 dried apricots, thinly sliced
½ cup raisins
¼ cup sugar, optional
½ teaspoon cinnamon, optional

In a medium saucepan over high heat, combine barley and 5 cups water. Cover and bring to a boil, then reduce heat to low and simmer until the barley is tender, about 30 minutes, adding more water if necessary to keep the barley covered. When the barley is ready, drain, reserving ½ cup of liquid (if there is not enough, add water to make ½ cup). Transfer the barley to a large bowl.

Meanwhile, bring small saucepan of water to the boil. Stir in poppy seeds, then remove from heat and let it stand, covered, for 30 minutes. In a dry skillet over moderate heat, toast almonds for about 4 minutes, shaking pan constantly, until browned and fragrant. Set aside.

In a fine-mesh strainer, drain the poppy seeds, then transfer to a food processor. Process until finely ground. Stir the reserved liquid, honey, and salt into the barley. Add toasted almonds, ground poppy seeds, apricots, and raisins, mixing well.

Preheat the oven to 325°F (163°C). Lightly butter an 8-inch square baking dish or 2-quart shallow casserole dish. Press barley mixture evenly into the dish. Bake for 20 minutes, then leave to cool. Cover, and chill overnight.

In a small bowl, whisk together sugar and cinnamon. Spoon chilled *kutia* into small bowls, sprinkle with the cinnamon-sugar mixture if desired, and serve. Serves six to eight.

E

N

Donetsk

ariupol

MAP OF UKRAINE

- Capital city
- Major town
▲ Mountain peak

Feet	Meters
16,500	5,000
9,900	3,000
6,600	2,000
3,300	1,000
1,650	500
660	200
0	0

ECONOMIC UKRAINE

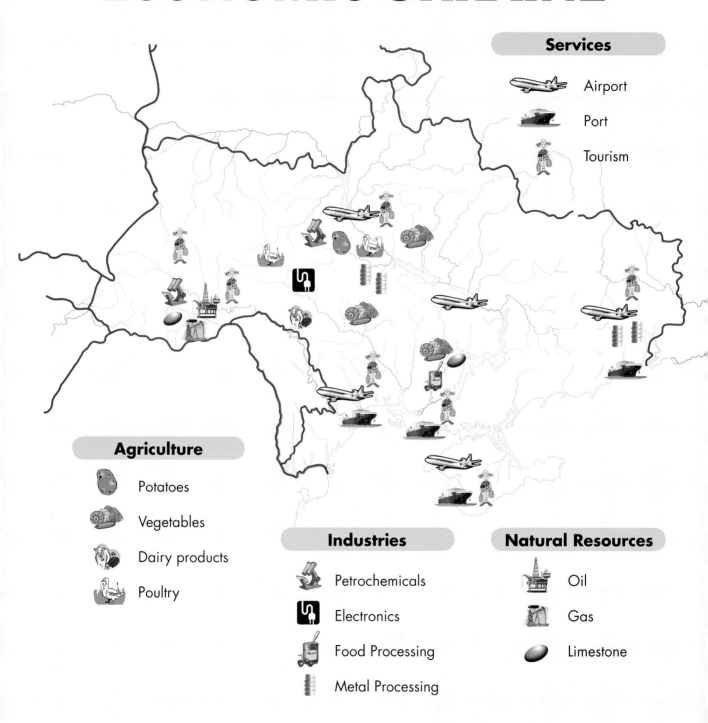

Services
- Airport
- Port
- Tourism

Agriculture
- Potatoes
- Vegetables
- Dairy products
- Poultry

Industries
- Petrochemicals
- Electronics
- Food Processing
- Metal Processing

Natural Resources
- Oil
- Gas
- Limestone

ABOUT
THE ECONOMY

OVERVIEW
Ukraine's rich black soil and its farms provide substantial quantities of meat, milk, grain, and vegetables to other countries. Its diversified heavy industry supplies unique equipment (such as large-diameter pipes) and raw materials to industrial and mining sites in other regions of the former Soviet Union. It depends on imports of energy, especially natural gas, to meet some 85 percent of its annual energy requirements.

GROSS DOMESTIC PRODUCT (GDP)
$364.3 billion (2006 estimate)

GDP SECTORS
Agriculture 17.5 percent, Industry 42.7 percent, Services 39.8 percent (2006 estimates)

WORKFORCE
22.3 million (2006 estimate)

INFLATION RATE
7.1 percent (2006 estimate)

CURRENCY
Hryvnia (UAH)
USD 1 = 5.11 UAH (August 2007)
Notes: 1, 2, 5,10, 20, 50, 100, 200
Coins (kopiykas): 1, 2, 5, 10, 25, 50

NATURAL RESOURCES
Iron ore, coal, manganese, natural gas, oil, salt, sulfur, graphite, titanium, magnesium, kaolin, nickel, mercury, timber, arable land

INDUSTRIAL PRODUCTS
Coal, electric power, ferrous and nonferrous metals, machinery and transportation equipment, chemicals, food processing (especially sugar)

AGRICULTURAL PRODUCTS
Grains, sugar beets, sunflower seeds, vegetables, beef, milk

UNEMPLOYMENT RATE
2.7 percent (officially registered); 6.7 percent (as calculated by the International Labor Organization) (2006 estimates)

ROADS
Total of 105,312 miles (169,447 km), paved 102,406 miles (164,772 km), unpaved 2,906 miles (4,675 km)

RAILWAYS
Total 13,967 miles (22,473 km), of which 5,749 miles (9,250 km) are electrified.

INTERNET ACCESSIBILITY
Internet users: 5.28 million (2005 estimate)
Internet hosts: 229,110 (2006 estimate)

CULTURAL UKRAINE

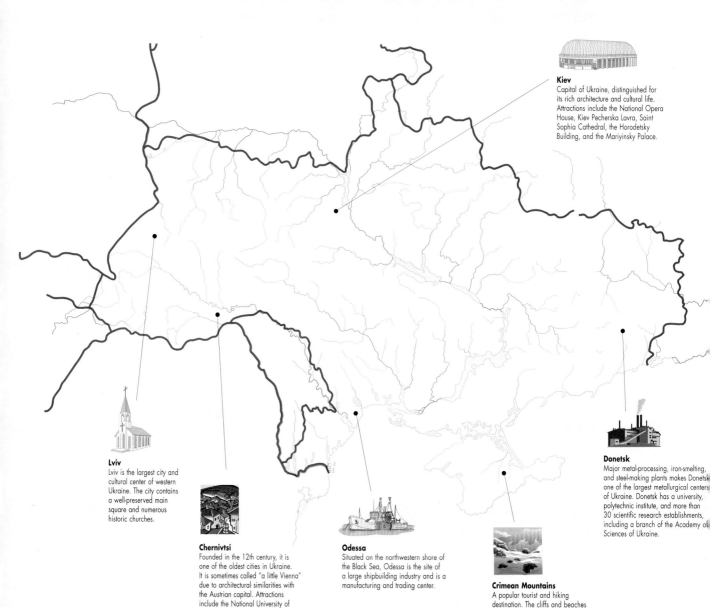

Kiev
Capital of Ukraine, distinguished for its rich architecture and cultural life. Attractions include the National Opera House, Kiev Pecherska Lavra, Saint Sophia Cathedral, the Horodetsky Building, and the Mariyinsky Palace.

Lviv
Lviv is the largest city and cultural center of western Ukraine. The city contains a well-preserved main square and numerous historic churches.

Chernivtsi
Founded in the 12th century, it is one of the oldest cities in Ukraine. It is sometimes called "a little Vienna" due to architectural similarities with the Austrian capital. Attractions include the National University of Chernivtsi and the Chernivtsi Drama Theater (a perfectly conserved art nouveau theater built in 1905).

Odessa
Situated on the northwestern shore of the Black Sea, Odessa is the site of a large shipbuilding industry and is a manufacturing and trading center.

Crimean Mountains
A popular tourist and hiking destination. The cliffs and beaches at Yalta also offer spectacular views of the Black Sea.

Donetsk
Major metal-processing, iron-smelting, and steel-making plants makes Donetsk one of the largest metallurgical centers of Ukraine. Donetsk has a university, polytechnic institute, and more than 30 scientific research establishments, including a branch of the Academy of Sciences of Ukraine.

ABOUT THE CULTURE

COUNTRY NAME
Ukraine

CAPITAL CITY
Kiev

FLAG
Two equal horizontal bands of azure (top) and golden yellow, representing grain fields under a blue sky.

OTHER IMPORTANT CITIES
Kharkiv, Dnipropetrovsk, Donetsk, Odessa, Lviv

POPULATION
46.3 million (2007)

ETHNIC GROUPS
Ukrainians, Russians, Belarussians, Moldovans, Hungarians, Bulgarians, Jews, Poles, Crimean Tatars

LIFE EXPECTANCY
Total average 67.88 years: male 62.16 years; female 73.96 years (2007 estimates)

BIRTHRATE
9.45 births per 1,000 Ukrainians (2007 estimate)

DEATH RATE
16.07 deaths per 1,000 Ukrainians (2007 estimate)

POPULATION GROWTH RATE
-0.675 percent (2007)

LITERACY RATE
Total 99.4 percent: male 99.7 percent; female 99.2 percent (2001 estimates)

MAJOR HOLIDAYS AND FESTIVALS
New Year's Day, Eastern Orthodox Christmas, Easter, Women's Day, Spring and Labor Days, Victory Day, Ukrainian Independence Day

RELIGIONS
Ukrainian Orthodox, Ukrainian Greek Catholic, Judaism, Roman Catholic, Islam

OFFICIAL LANGUAGES
Ukrainian, Russian

LEADERS IN POLITICS
Viktor Yushchenko, president of Ukraine; Viktor Yanukovych, prime minister

LEADERS IN THE ARTS
Taras Shevchenko, Mykola Hohol, Ivan Franko (writers and poets); Kykola Lysenko, Tetyana Yablonska, Olaksandr Dovzhenko (culture and the arts)

TIME LINE

IN UKRAINE	IN THE WORLD
	A.D. 600 Height of Mayan civilization
A.D. 911–988 Prince Vladimir of Kiev accepts Byzantine Orthodoxy. Beginning of Russian Christianity.	
	1000 The Chinese perfect gunpowder and begin to use it in warfare.
1237 Mongols conquer Russian lands. Mongols under Batu Khan occupy and destroy Kiev.	
	1558–1603 Reign of Elizabeth I of England
1654 Union of Ukraine and Russia announced.	**1620** Pilgrims sail the *Mayflower* to America.
1709 Peter the Great defeats Charles XII at Poltava in Ukraine, ending the Swedish empire.	
	1776 U.S. Declaration of Independence
1783 Catherine the Great annexes the Crimea to the Russian Empire. Tatars are 83 percent of the residents.	
	1789–99 The French Revolution
1794 Ukraine's port city of Odessa is founded.	
1853–56 The Crimean War.	
1890 Vaslav Nijinsky, considered the world's greatest ballet dancer, is born in Kiev.	**1861** The U.S. Civil War begins.
	1914 World War I begins.
1917–21 Ukraine declares independence following the collapse of the Russian Empire. The Ukrainian Soviet Socialist Republic is established.	
1932 About 7 million peasants perish in famine during Stalin's collectivization campaign.	
1937 Mass executions and deportations as Stalin launches purge against intellectuals.	**1939** World War II begins.

IN UKRAINE	IN THE WORLD
1941–44 Germany occupies the country. More than 5 million Ukrainians die fighting the Nazis, including most of Ukraine's 1.5 million Jews.	
1945 Allied victory in World War II leads to Soviet annexation of western Ukrainian lands.	**1945** The United States drops atomic bombs on Hiroshima and Nagasaki.
	1949 The North Atlantic Treaty Organization (NATO) is formed.
1954 Armed resistance to Soviet rule ends with defeat of Ukrainian Insurgent Army.	**1966** The Chinese Cultural Revolution
1986 Nuclear power disaster at Chernobyl.	
1988 Prominent writers and intellectuals set up Ukrainian People's Movement for Restructuring (Rukh).	
1991 Ukraine declares independence. About 250,000 exiled Crimean Tatars return to Crimea following collapse of Soviet Union.	**1991** Breakup of the Soviet Union
	1997 Hong Kong is returned to China.
2000 Chernobyl nuclear power plant is shut down and sealed.	
2001 Pope John Paul II makes his first visit to Ukraine amid protests by Orthodox Christians in Ukraine and Russia.	**2001** Terrorists crash planes in New York, Washington, D.C., and Pennsylvania.
2002 Ukraine announces formal bid to join NATO. Mass protests demanding resignation of President Kuchma, who is accused of corruption and misrule.	
2003 Border dispute with Moscow over a causeway project across the Kerch Strait between Russia and the Ukrainian island of Tuzla.	**2003** War in Iraq begins.

GLOSSARY

bandura (bahn-DOO-rah)
A multistringed, irregularly-shaped musical instrument.

bohomaz (boh-hoh-MAHZ)
An artist specializing in religious designs.

borscht (BORSH)
A classic Ukrainian soup made with red beets, meat, and other ingredients.

chornozem (chor-noh-ZEM)
Black Ukrainian soil.

hetman (HET-mahn)
The title given to prominent Kozak leaders in the 15th to 18th centuries.

hopak (hoh-PAHK)
An energetic dance performed by men.

horilka (hoh-RIL-kah)
Ukrainian vodka.

hryvna (HRIV-nah)
The monetary unit (UAH) in Kievan Rus, reintroduced in 1996.

karbovanets (kahr-BOH-vah-nets)
The temporary currency from 1992 to 1996.

kistka (KIST-kah)
The tool used for drawing wax patterns on Easter eggs.

kobzar (kob-ZAHR)
A folk singer or bard.

Kozak (koh-ZAHK)
Cossack, a Ukrainian military man of the 15th to 18th centuries.

krashanka (KRAH-shahn-kah)
A Ukrainian Easter egg dyed in one bright color.

Lavra (LAH-vrah)
The monastery of the highest importance under the direct jurisdiction of the patriarch of the Ukrainian Orthodox Church.

militsya (mih-LIH-tsiah)
Police.

oblast (OB-lahst)
State or province.

pyrohy (pih-roh-HIH)
Pastries with various fillings, such as meat, vegetables, or sweets.

pysanka (PIH-sahn-kah)
A Ukrainian Easter egg with an artistic multicolored design.

trembita (trem-BEE-tah)
A wind instrument used in the Carpathian Mountains.

varenyki (vah-REH-nih-kih)
Dumplings with various fillings.

FURTHER INFORMATION

BOOKS

Alexievich, Svetlana. *Voices from Chernobyl: The Oral History of a Nuclear Disaster.* New York: Picador, 2006.

Baltiia, Druk, ed. *Touring Lviv.* Kiev, Ukraine, 2005.

Baltiia, Druk, ed. *Touring Odessa.* Kiev, Ukraine, 2004.

Derlemenko, E. A. *Parky Ukrainy: Fotoal'bom (Parks of Ukraine).* Kiev, Ukraine: Baltiia Druk, 2006.

Hodges, Linda and Chumak, George. *Language and Travel Guide to Ukraine.* New York: Hippocrene Books, 2004.

Isajiw, Wsevolod, ed. *Society in Transition: Social Change in Ukraine in Western Perspectives.* Toronto: Canadian Scholars ' Press, Inc., 2003.

Johnstone, Sarah. *Ukraine (Lonely Planet Travel Guides).* Oakland, CA Lonely Planet Publications, 2005.

WEB SITES

All Ukrainian Population Census 2001. www.ukrcensus.gov.ua/eng/

Energy Information Administration, Ukraine. www.eia.doe.gov/emeu/cabs/Ukraine/Background.html

European Neighborhood Policy. http://ec.europa.eu/world/enp/documents_en.htm

External Relations—The EU's relations with Ukraine. http://ec.europa.eu/external_relations/ukraine/intro/index.htm

Migration Information Source. http://migrationinformation.net/Feature/print.cfm?ID=533

Ukraine Government portal (in Ukranian). www.kmu.gov.ua

Ukraine Political Parties. www.globalsecurity.org

Ukrainian Public Mission . www.ukrcognita.com.ua

U.S.-EU Summit Political Progress Report 2007. www.whitehouse.gov/news/ releases/2007/04/20070430-9.html

World Bank. www.worldbank.org.ua

BIBLIOGRAPHY

Farley, Marta Pisetska. *Festive Ukrainian Cooking*. Pittsburgh, PA: University of Pittsburgh Press, 1990.

Shevchenko, Taras. *Selected Works: Poetry and Prose*. Moscow: Progress Publishers, 1979.

———. *Taras Shevchenko, the Poet of Ukraine: Selected Poems*. Jersey City, NJ: Ukrainian National Association, 1945.

INDEX